Just Three Days
From Heartbreak to Hope

Tim and Serena Howell

**Compiled and Written by
Angela Welch Prusia**

Cover created by:
Randy Hill Creative
P.O. Box 17264, Salem, OR 97304
503.507.1228
www.hilldesignstudios.com

Published in Beaverton, Oregon, by Good Book Publishing.
www.goodbookpublishing.com
V1.1

Printed in the United States of America

Table of Contents

Acknowledgements   9

Introduction from Wayne Tesch   11

The Beginning   13

Part One   23
  A Giant Killing:
  David and Goliath

Part Two   77
  Illuminating Our Lives with Truth:
  The Story of Joseph

Part Three   155
  A Well-Beaten Path:
  Daniel and the Lions' Den

Part Four   221
  Gutsy Conversations:
  Jonah and the Whale

About the Author   287

Acknowledgements

As Teen Reach Adventure Camp celebrates 10 years, we would like to acknowledge those who have made the dream a reality.

- God. Giver of life and dreams, we love you.
- Our parents, Phil and Ruby Howell, the late Wanda Voigtel and Rudy and Kris Voigtel.
- Our daughters, Morgan and Mackenzie Howell.
- Tim Rote, thank you for investing in the vision, along with all those who've given and the many who faithfully invest in the future.
- Wayne and Diane Tesch for inspiring us to serve the orphans of our society and mentoring us.
- Friends that made it all happen: Donald and Gayle Brown, Dennis Roach, Ted and Sharon Shafer, John and Kathie Taggart, Ryan Taggart, Trevor and Christy Taggart, Lloyd and Colleen West, Dan and Sharla Wyland.
- The numerous T.R.A.C. Directors and Staff.
- Hope Unlimited, Inc. board members, thank you for your time and wisdom.
- All T.R.A.C. Sherwood volunteers who have helped expand the vision nationally.

- The pastors and congregation of Horizon Community Church.

We treasure each of you!

For Him,
Tim & Serena Howell

The author wishes to thank God for His faithfulness. Without Him and the support of her husband, kids and parents, Ben and Pat Welch, *Just Three Days: From Heartbreak to Hope* would not be a reality. Angela is also grateful to Tim and Serena Howell for their obedience to God's call, as well as her New Life Assembly family, Pastor Bob and Connie Wine and the Kearney T.R.A.C. team for joining the wild ride. Special thanks to Kim Stokely for her editing expertise and Daren Lindley, Melody Davis and the staff at Good Book Publishing.

Introduction

I met Tim Howell in 1996. After I spoke at Grace (now Horizon) Community Church, Tim stopped me to say, "Someday I believe we will be working together."

A year later, after Tim helped with the church's first Royal Family KIDS Camp, I received a dinner invitation. Tim wanted to help expand the ministry of Royal Family KIDS.

Between Serena's warm hospitality and Tim's "grillin' prowess," I had a great time. Their daughters, Morgan and Mackenzie, sat at the table telling jokes. Laughter and joy punctuated the conversation. The evening flew by.

From 1997-1999, Tim and I had lunch meetings with pastors and church leaders in Portland, Oregon, Spokane and Richland, Washington, and Anchorage, Alaska. We enjoyed our time carrying the message of hope for foster children.

In 2000, Tim and Serena attended a camp directors' training for Royal Family KIDS in Houghton, New York. It was there the two of them shared with me the concept of T.R.A.C. — working with the graduates of Royal Family KIDS to follow them through their teen years.

I have known this couple for close to 15 years. I marvel at their dedication and perseverance. I am amazed at the blending of their business and ministry skills to help the foster teens of our nation.

As you read the stories, you will be marking a milestone in the ministry — 10 years of faithful service to teens in foster care. Stories of Matthew, Levi, Leila and others have captured my heart.

When you read this book, keep a tissue close by. It is amazing what can be accomplished in three days when God is directing the life. Moments matter.

T.R.A.C. is filled with such events — God's people taking time to make a difference in the lives of teens. Oh, the joy — the transformations!

Celebrate 10 years with Tim and Serena.

May God continue to bless Teen Reach Adventure Camp to be a blessing.

Wayne Tesch
Co-Founder, Royal Family KIDS

The Beginning

Everyone would ask me, "What is your favorite thing about camp?" All I ever had to say was that I don't have a favorite. It has been my first time being here, and the first day, I knew I wouldn't want to leave. Everyone has been helpful, kind, peaceful and hopeful. Their faces are all imprinted in my heart, soul and mind. I will never forget these three days at camp! I love camp.

Can three days impact a life?

Ask the teenager who penned the words above. This girl, like others in foster care whose stories fill these pages, experienced three fun-filled days at one of the many gender-specific Teen Reach Adventure Camps across the country.

Tim and Serena Howell founded T.R.A.C. to provide hope and a future to at-risk teens ages 12-15. For many wards of the state, life is a series of changes from one temporary home to another. Leaving behind siblings, special pets and favorite belongings manifests itself in behavioral and medical issues which make attending other summer camps difficult. Multiple medications for depression, mood swings, anxiety, hyperactivity and insomnia are common among T.R.A.C. campers. Life is a minefield where survival trumps fun.

Just Three Days

❧❧❧

The dream of serving abused children was awakened in Tim Howell on a spring Sunday in 1996. Sitting in a pew at Grace (now Horizon) Community Church in Tualatin, Oregon, Tim listened to Wayne Tesch, co-founder of Royal Family KIDS, talk about ministering to foster kids through summer camp.

"Maybe someone here today will respond to God's call," Wayne's deep voice boomed across the audience. "Perhaps God is asking you to help a child find hope for the future."

Time stood still around Tim.

"Experiencing God's love in the cathedral of the outdoors changes lives," Wayne's voice trailed off.

Tim's heartbeat thumped in the silence, and he heard God whisper. *You need to help.*

After the service, Tim spoke to Wayne. As a licensed counselor, he would start by volunteering as a therapist for the Tualatin camp. Deep down, Tim knew Royal Family KIDS would change the course of his life.

As Tim expected, the week at camp touched him deeply. He wanted to do more, but doubt set in, so he waited to share the stirring inside him until his wife's birthday. "If Serena wavers at all," Tim bargained with God, "I'll know the call I heard a year ago wasn't your voice."

After dinner at Timberline Lodge, Tim tried to mask his nervousness as he casually brought up the topic. "I feel

The Beginning

God calling us to help Wayne Tesch expand Royal Family KIDS Camps on a national level. What do you think?"

Serena didn't hesitate. "Sounds like we need to be obedient."

Tim exhaled. God had answered his prayer. It was time to invite Wayne to dinner.

ॐॐॐ

Serena joined Tim as a volunteer at the Tualatin camp, and Tim helped Wayne plant more Royal Family KIDS Camps in Oregon, Washington and Alaska. Two years later, the couple headed to directors' training in Houghton, New York. For a week, they studied a Royal Family KIDS Camp in action with other directors-in-training. Observing foster kids reclaim their childhoods as they romped around the campground, splashed in the lake and spent time with camp grandparents and loving "big campers" (counselors) was overwhelming. The Howells returned to their dorm room after the graduation ceremony, broken and emotionally spent.

They collapsed on their bunk beds, both staring at the ceiling. Neither said a word.

"Watching those kids graduate tore me up," Tim finally said.

Serena's eyes still stung. She pictured the teary 11 year olds on stage, trying to keep a stiff upper lip as they realized they wouldn't return to camp. Many had come for five years.

"There needs to be another camp for the graduates." Her voice caught. "It just seems so impossible." They had two young daughters and a fast-growing counseling business.

"That's how I've been feeling," Tim confessed. "But I'm so confused. Why would God call us to develop more Royal Family KIDS Camps, then break our hearts for the graduates?"

Once again, they prayed for the next step.

❧❧❧

Four years earlier, Tim and Serena began looking at land outside of Portland, Oregon. When a deal fell through, a friend mentioned property in Sherwood needing a quick sale. Incredibly, the home on the five-acre plot matched the dream home Serena had sketched. Their house sold in two weeks, and they purchased the place in Sherwood on contract and finished six months of work in two. One of the first items to hang on the wall was a poem written by Tim's grandfather when they'd bought their first home:

When a House Becomes a Home

It takes LOVE, UNDERSTANDING and TRUST …
All of this, truly is a must.

The Beginning

A house becomes a HOME where LOVE abounds.
The SINGING and the LAUGHTER,
such beautiful sounds.

May this house you have purchased be
all of this and more.
May the hurting and the friendless find
welcome at your door.

As you minister to their needs with
God's Word and with Prayer.
In this house you have purchased,
may they find comfort there.

ॡॡॡ

The prophetic words unfolded as Tim and Serena took a step of faith and began to develop two separate gender camps for abused teenagers. A training model provided by Wayne and Diane Tesch served as a stepping off point, and Hope Unlimited, Inc., a public non-profit, was born.

One Indian summer day, the Howells shared their dream with Tim Rote, a good friend who had a compassionate heart for hurting teens.

"What's the budget?" he asked after listening intently.

Tim and Serena exchanged a look of surprise. Serena shared the printout of the budget they'd estimated a week earlier.

Their friend pulled out his checkbook and wrote a

check for $10,000. "I will give you this on one condition: These camps need to serve abused teens next summer. Is that going to be a problem?"

Tim and Serena didn't waste time. They started work on their property the following weekend. Friends — too numerous to list — gave up weekends to help clear vine maple and wild blackberry bushes. Volunteers also leveled areas that would later house tents and Cross Talk, a time of worship and teaching about Biblical characters who overcame difficulties with God's help.

God's hand of protection was clearly evident. One afternoon, Tim and two friends piled debris on a fire when the wind shifted. As soon as the track hoe operator had put down the safety protector, a shot rang out, instantly shattering the glass on the machine. An old bullet had been left in the forest and ignited in the heat.

Tim and the men blinked in disbelief, realizing how narrowly they'd missed a fatal blow.

ॐॐॐ

God was growing the dream in others, too, like friends and volunteers Don and Gayle Brown. Tim did not know Don's own background mirrored the lives Hope Unlimited, Inc. would later serve. The youngest of seven kids, Don watched his mother fight with various boyfriends over rent or grocery money wasted on booze. By age 12, Don was regularly picking up his mother from the local bar.

The Beginning

Summer camp changed the course of Don's life. When the YMCA offered him a scholarship, he met other teens like himself who struggled with fear and lack of confidence. For the first time in his life, Don experienced unconditional love from his counselor and other staff. He shot his first bull's eye, caught his first crawdad, rode horses, hiked and heard about the love of Jesus. At camp at age 16, he asked Jesus into his heart. This decision grounded him when his mother abandoned him the following year. He credits camp for setting him on the right path — finishing school, working hard and a 32-year marriage — so working with T.R.A.C. was a perfect fit. Don and Tim were still digging tent railing when the first bus of campers rolled into Sherwood in the summer of 2002.

అఅఅ

After the first year of T.R.A.C., Tim and Serena felt something was missing from the overall program. Three days didn't leave much time for trust to develop. A challenge course would help connect campers as a team and build self value, but the Howells weren't sure how to begin.

Enter Dennis Roach from Union Gospel Mission in Spokane, Washington, whom the Howells had met when they helped expand Royal Family KIDS Camps.

Dennis made an unplanned stop in Sherwood one evening that fall.

After friendly conversation in front of a fire, Dennis confided feeling a prompting to visit. "I don't really know why I'm here. I could've driven home a much shorter way." He looked from Tim to Serena. "Is there something I can do for you?"

Tim shared their desire for a challenge course at T.R.A.C.

"Isn't that interesting?" A glimmer shined in Dennis' eye. "I happen to be a certified builder and trainer of trust courses."

Dennis soon designed the T.R.A.C. challenge course program, which has proven successful in breaking down walls of distrust through team-building activities. Facilitators frame challenges in scenarios which stretch campers to work together. The challenges increase in difficulty over the three days from the "teepee shuffle" and "minefield" to the "spider web" and "trust fall." Debriefing helps campers process their thoughts and feelings, a skill many lack.

෨෨෨

Seeing the impact three days made in the lives of foster teens, two friends and volunteers Lloyd and Colleen West saw a larger vision.

"You should do this on a national level," Lloyd told Tim over coffee on their deck.

He and his wife had adopted two kids, so they knew firsthand how much these children needed hope and stable adults to speak encouragement into their lives.

"No." Tim shook his head. Running camp had been a huge undertaking. He and Serena couldn't imagine running a large-scale ministry.

Lloyd kept pressing, and others encouraged the two to develop a model that could operate both nationally and internationally. With a great deal of guidance from the Tesches and Lloyd West, the Howells agreed, and T.R.A.C. held its first national directors' training in 2005.

God had a dream to share, and it was bigger than Tim and Serena could ever imagine.

ॐॐॐ

As Teen Reach Adventure Camp celebrates its 10th anniversary, 28 separate gender camps operate in nine states across the United States. In the summer of 2012, 38 separate gender camps will operate in 11 states, providing hope to more than 1,000 abused teenagers. In 2009, Hope Unlimited, Inc. also launched **T.R.A.C.***life,* a mentoring program which pairs T.R.A.C. campers with T.R.A.C. staff for a yearlong mentoring relationship.

The Howells and the board of Hope Unlimited, Inc. continue to dream. They envision other ministries for foster teens, including forever homes, self-sustaining ranch/camp facilities that would house aged-out foster teens year-round. An endowment fund and succession plan are being established to ensure the long-term stability of the organization.

Just Three Days

Two verses underscore the mission of Hope Unlimited, Inc. Jeremiah 29:11: "'For I know the plans I have for you,' declares the Lord, 'plans to prosper you and not to harm you, plans to give you hope and a future.'" Not only does God have a hope and a future for the fatherless in the foster care system, He will renew their strength as stated in Isaiah 40:30-31a. "Even youths grow tired and weary, and young men stumble and fall; but those who hope in the Lord will renew their strength."

Can three days impact a life?

Ten years of Teen Reach Adventure Camp is proving three days does make a difference, turning heartbreak to hope.

For those who wish to serve God by partnering with Hope Unlimited, Inc., please contact:

Hope Unlimited, Inc.
P.O. Box 1589
Sherwood, OR 97140
503-625-1299
FAX: 503-625-2863
www.teenreachadventurecamp.org

Part One
A Giant Killing: David and Goliath
"David, a man after God's own heart."

Each year, Cross Talk focuses on one character from the Bible — David, Joseph, Daniel or Jonah — who faced difficult situations and emerged victoriously with God's help.

During the first year, campers learn about David, a shepherd boy who faced a giant named Goliath. Like David, teens at T.R.A.C. encounter Goliaths which seem impossible to slay. Abandonment haunts them, and abuse robs them of healthy relationships. Rejection by their biological parents is a giant which screams, "You're worthless. You're nothing. Who could love you?"

The study of David teaches Psalm 29:11. "The Lord gives strength to His people; the Lord blesses His people with peace." Campers begin to see facing giants is easier with God.

The Dollar

After Tim Howell shared the T.R.A.C. dream at his church in Oregon, a long line of people waited to talk to him.

A small girl caught Tim's attention. Ali was only 5 or 6 years old, and Tim knew she was going through a tough time with her parents' divorce.

"Hey, there." Tim bent down, so he was at Ali's eye level.

She thrust out a dollar. "I don't have a lot to give, but I want you to have this."

Tim pocketed the dollar and placed one of his own in the donation bucket. He would keep this dollar in his desk drawer as a reminder of the childlike faith Jesus treasures.

Years later, when the giant of discouragement looms and the dream seems too unreachable, Tim pulls out the child's dollar. God gives him strength, and Tim presses on to minister to the hurting.

The Three Giants

Dale, camp grandpa at Kearney, Nebraska, T.R.A.C., stood up from his table in the dining room to wish the boys goodbye. The clink of silverware quieted as campers stopped eating to listen. "I have to leave after breakfast because it'll be too hot to travel with the horses later."

A few campers groaned.

Dale cleared his throat. "I've lived longer than most of you've been alive. And I've learned something I want to share with you before I go."

Expectation filled the air.

"We've been talking about David this weekend." Dale searched the faces of the boys, compassion etched on his own.

"I've faced a lot of giants in my time. Some I've slain. Others got the better of me."

Several eyes widened.

"What I've learned is that we face three giants." Dale held up his hand and counted with his fingers. "One: our own rebellion and independence. Two: fear. And three: unforgiveness."

The boys were quiet as they processed his words.

Dale smiled. "You know my horse, Foxy?"

Many heads nodded. The boys loved Dale's mare and her foal, Prince.

"Prince was real sick when he was born." Dale paused. "He would've died without medication. He hated me putting tablets down his throat, but his mama reassured him. Foxy trusted me because I'd raised her since she was a baby."

Dale choked up. "That's a metaphor for us. If I'm God, and you're the colt, Mama is the crowd you hang with."

Dale let his words sink in.

"You kill more giants when you hang with a crowd that points you to God."

Understanding registered on many of the campers' faces.

"Look at the volunteers around you, boys." Heads turned toward the adults in the room.

"Find people who love and trust God like the staff here at T.R.A.C."

Dale's smile reached his eyes. "Do that, and you'll be a giant slayer."

Just Three Days

Dear T.R.A.C.,

Thank you so much for letting me come to camp. You opened me up when I was just about to give up, knowing that God put me here for a reason ... I had a BLAST and can't wait till next year.

Thank you so much.

God bless,
Mia

From the Same Tribe

James grinned as soon as he got off the Scio, Oregon, T.R.A.C. bus and spied Ted. The two knew each other from Royal Family KIDS Camp where Coach Ted organized the games.

"You hiding a water balloon?" Ted narrowed his eyes, searching James for any concealed balloons. The happy-go-lucky teenager was famous for nailing Ted.

James stuck out empty hands and laughed. "Just wait till later."

The campers headed toward three new cabins, each fitted with permanent bunks, carpet and electricity. Volunteers used materials purchased through grant money from the Siletz Tribe to build the cabins.

"Did you see the plaques?" James pulled Ted toward the nearest one. The two had discovered they were from the same Native American tribe at an earlier camp. "The cabins are from our tribe."

Ted and James admired the 9x6-inch wooden plaque over the door. "The Siletz Tribe" was engraved on a brass plate.

Pride radiated from James' dark eyes. "Our tribe did this."

James turned 16 the following year, so he was too old for camp, but Gary and Palma, the directors, invited him to a skit performed by their church based on the movie *Facing the Giants*.

The kid with the huge smile and long dark hair had shot up and thinned out.

"My mom's out of prison now," James told the directors. "She has custody of a few of us." Five of her seven kids had been campers at Royal Family KIDS or T.R.A.C., so the family was close to Gary and Palma's hearts.

"T.R.A.C. and Royal Family KIDS brought stability to my life," James shared. "Thank you."

Palma squeezed Gary's hand. He'd quit his job as an engineer consultant to be home more for T.R.A.C., and she'd joined Tim and Serena after 35 years of nursing to plant camps across the country. Even their 10 acres was dedicated to the ministry. The reason: kids like James and a chance to share hope with the future.

The Dress

Music by the group Pink reverberated through the air at Glendale, Arizona, T.R.A.C. Tired campers perked up, their lips moving to the song. When the last words faded, Joy, the Cross Talk teacher, fastened the lyrics, written on a large piece of paper, to the nearest cabin door.

"I'm going to play this a second time," she explained. "And I want you to underline any phrase that describes how you feel."

The song hardly began when girls rushed forward in a frenzied mob, markers in hand. By the end, nearly every phrase was underlined, many multiple times.

My parents hated me.
I can't do nothin' right.
I wanna be somebody else.

The next day, Joy summed up the teaching on David. "God is your source for strength and peace," she said, dipping a brush into red paint and covering the underlined phrases. While the song finished, Joy then painted a purple cross over the red background.

"What do you think this symbolizes?"

Jordan, a petite girl with blond hair, didn't hesitate. "It represents Christ's blood covering our sins and reminding us where our value comes from. It comes from God."

Several staff eyed one another. The change in Jordan was remarkable. At age 15, she had been in 20 foster homes. Three failed adoptions left her angry. She'd come to camp confused and struggling with giants of body issues and self-esteem.

Jordan surprised the staff again with her heartfelt prayer.

"Dear God," Jordan began. "Thank You for this wonderful time we've all had up here. May You give us strength and comfort us. Please help us to remember what we've learned and apply it to our lives — to remember how You see us and not how other people see us. I pray this in Your name. Amen."

A few months later, Kelli, T.R.A.C. director, visited the group home where Jordan lived.

"We saw a major change after camp," the group home leader shared. "Jordan doesn't lose her temper like before. Now she goes into her room when she's angry and puts on her dress."

"It reminds me God loves me no matter what anyone else thinks," Jordan told Kelli.

Kelli had to leave the room to cry. She could see Jordan at the Princess Program, dressed in a silky white formal with spaghetti straps. The girl looked like an angel.

Three days can change a life.

Part One: David and Goliath

The Cat Man

The boys called Rich the Cat Man because he drove an Arctic Cat ATV to haul water, snacks and other supplies around camp. Tall prairie grass parted in his wake. A big guy at more than 6 feet tall and 300 pounds, the Cat Man was a favorite. The campers at Manhattan, Kansas, T.R.A.C. loved him.

During the final challenge — the trust fall — campers surrounded a 3 ½-foot tree stump. One boy after another donned a blindfold, climbed onto the stump and fell backward into the arms of his teammates.

The familiar sound of the ATV approached.

"Rich, you gotta do it!" Pablo called out. He was beaming from his own success. Not only had he accomplished the trust fall, he'd scaled the wall. "It's so awesome!"

The Cat Man shook his head. "I don't think so."

"I trusted you on the wall, Rich," Pablo reminded him. "Won't you trust me?"

What could he say? The Cat Man sighed in resignation. He got off the ATV and climbed onto the stump with shaky legs. Sweat beaded his forehead. "I'm too big," he protested. "I'm going to hurt someone."

"We got you," Pablo told him. "Trust us."

Rich leaned back … and the campers caught him.

After camp, Lisa, the co-director, called Rich to check on him. "You were so quiet during staff debriefing," she said. "Are you okay?"

"Yeah." His voice caught. "I just had to go home and cry."

Lisa understood. She was struggling herself. Three foster brothers — Jay, Chris and Colton — had warmed their way into her heart. They worked long hours for their foster family's roofing business, and camp was a chance for them to be boys.

Colton, the newest to the family, had lost his dad, and his mother was recently incarcerated. The hardness melted as he flew down the spring-fed waterslide at camp. When the Cross Talk teacher encouraged campers to pick up river rocks and throw their giants over the hill, Colton and his foster brothers had lobbed the stones far into the distance.

The Cat Man conquered his fear. Now Lisa had to let go of the giant called doubt and trust God to help Colton and the other campers slay their Goliaths.

Who Are You People?

Cindy, the director of T.R.A.C. in The Woodlands, Texas, answered the phone on the second ring. "Hello. This is Cindy."

Brandy, a supervisor with Child Protective Services in Brownwood, Texas, didn't waste time with a greeting. "Who are you people?"

Cindy held the phone to her ear, not sure how to answer. Brandy had driven seven hours to bring eight girls to camp. *Was she regretting that decision now? Would Brandy back out the following weekend with the boys she planned to bring?*

Brandy didn't wait for Cindy to answer. "We just stopped for a bathroom break on our way home, and Sammy has talked nonstop for two hours."

Cindy remembered the beautiful girl who'd conquered her giant at camp. Prior to T.R.A.C., she'd been terrified of horses.

"Seriously," Brandy asked again. "I've never heard Sammy say more than a sentence or two, and she's smiling and laughing. What have you done to these kids?"

"Nothing, really." Cindy tried to swallow the lump in her throat. "Just loved them."

Just Three Days

Dear T.R.A.C.,

My foster daughter came back (from camp) on fire and excited about God's word. She shared of the healing taking place in her life. She no longer blames God for her mother's death. You truly blessed her more than (you) may ever know.

Thank you,
P.F.

Friends

"I hate everyone," Caden announced on the challenge course the first day of Kearney, Nebraska, T.R.A.C. "There's no reason to trust anyone."

Day 2, his attitude hadn't changed.

The final day, Caden stood with his group in front of the 10-foot wall they'd successfully scaled. Evergreens shaded them from the summer heat as they took time to debrief.

"What walls do we have in life?" Jason, the facilitator, asked the campers.

Fear.

The past.

Drugs and alcohol.

Every camper mentioned a struggle they needed to overcome.

"I don't have any friends." Caden surprised Jason by opening up. Raw pain etched his face.

"I'm your friend." One of the campers jumped in without hesitating.

"Me, too," another answered.

Soon every teen affirmed Caden.

"Sounds like you have friends here." Jason met Caden's

eyes. "Why don't you think you have friends back home?"

Caden gulped. "Because I'm mean."

Jason's eyes softened. "Sounds like that's something you can change."

Staff received the following note covered in smiley faces from Caden:

> Thank you, T.R.A.C., for a fun time and the memories and teaching me about God. And thanks for letting me come, making me trust others.

A different young man boarded the bus for home, armed with truth to slay his giants of loneliness and isolation.

The Harlee Wall

"Who wants to be the first ever to scale the new camp wall?" Gary, the facilitator at Scio, Oregon, T.R.A.C., asked the girls.

Tucked in the woods, the challenge course provided a reprieve from the summer heat.

"No way," a petite girl refused, listening to the giant of doubt.

"But you girls are the first group. We just built it."

"I'm too short." Harlee frowned. "I can't get over that." She was in the middle of another round of protest when the team picked her up and hoisted her over the wall. She stood on top, beaming.

During debriefing, Harlee was still shocked. "No way could I do it, and you guys helped me!"

A few months later, Gary saw Harlee with her siblings at a Royal Family KIDS Christmas dinner.

"Hey, Harlee," Gary greeted her. "How you doing?"

She gave him a card she made at one of the activity centers.

"Can I share something with you?" Gary asked.

Harlee looked into his face with big eyes.

"God's going to use you and the soft heart He gave you." He paused. "You remember the wall?"

She lit up.

"I named it *The Harlee Wall.*"

"No, you didn't?!" Harlee was ecstatic.

"Yep. You were the first one over." A lump lodged in Gary's throat. "*The Harlee Wall* just fits."

Best Day

At 6 feet tall and 200 pounds, Levi lacked confidence. When his counselor at the Sherwood, Oregon, camp asked Levi to participate in the variety show that evening, he shook his head. "I can't."

At the Nitro challenge, Levi struggled to hang on to the rope because of his size. His entire team shouted encouragement and worked together to help him conquer the giant of defeat.

When Levi made it, a grin spread to his ears. "This is the best day of my life."

That night, a confident Levi ran onto the stage. Under a canopy of evergreens stretching to the sky, he belted out a song that wowed staff and campers alike. The smile never left his face.

A Giant Called Diabetes

Weeks before camp started, Sandy was still short of male counselors for Tyler, Texas, T.R.A.C. She and Nancy, her co-director, met together to discuss the situation.

"Have you heard back from David?" Nancy asked. The science teacher who'd volunteered with Royal Family KIDS would be perfect.

"He was still looking at his schedule," Sandy answered.

A knock on the door interrupted them. Sandy raised her eyebrows and eyed Nancy. Late morning on a weekday was a strange time for visitors.

"David!" Nancy exclaimed in surprise. "We were just talking about you."

"I was out running errands and thought I'd drop this by in person." David smiled, handing over his application. "I can help at T.R.A.C. this year."

Sandy clapped. "Oh, you're an answer to prayer."

Nancy asked him about Alvin, a camper with diabetes. "Would you care if we paired you together?"

David agreed without hesitation.

At camp, the redheaded, freckle-faced teen proved to be sharp, especially when it came to his medical issues with diabetes. He faithfully poked his finger to test his sugar levels and didn't flinch when he got his insulin shots. But like most teens, Alvin liked sweets. He tested the boundaries at camp and played a dangerous game, taking higher doses of insulin to compensate for the extra sugar he ate.

When David confronted him, Alvin whined. "It's not fair. I'm the only one who has to deal with this."

"Actually," David countered, "I teach at a school where four kids have diabetes, too."

"Really?"

David nodded. "You know how we've been talking about facing our giants?"

Alvin nodded.

"Diabetes is your giant, and you are the only one who can fight it."

Alvin mulled over the idea. By the end of camp, he'd embraced the idea. He realized his food choices gave him a certain amount of control over his diabetes, and he felt empowered.

"I've made more friends at camp than my whole life." Alvin beamed. "I don't feel different here. I'm accepted."

Just Three Days

Dear T.R.A.C.,

Thank you for all you have done. You have made my life fun. You have shown me that there are people out there that love you. The past three days changed my life forever. Thank you so much. Hope to see you next year. Thank you for all you gave me.

Love you forever,
Rochelle

Minefield

Laura stared at the objects scattered on the ground at Manhattan, Kansas, T.R.A.C.

"This is a minefield," the facilitator explained. "Any volunteers?"

"I'll do it." The first-year camper didn't hesitate. Crooked teeth revealed a bright smile.

"I'm going to blindfold you." He tied a bandana around Laura's eyes. "Can you see?"

Laura shook her head, and another girl volunteered to navigate.

The facilitator whispered something to the other girls, then squared Laura's shoulders and pointed her away from the first object. "Since you can't see, you have to listen to your coach as you walk through this minefield. Ready?"

Laura grinned. Suddenly the other girls started yelling different messages in an effort to distract her. "Go left!" "Go right!"

Laura took a step, and her knees buckled. Earlier she'd shared her giant of abandonment at Cross Talk. "I felt so alone when my parents told me they didn't want me anymore." Now Laura sobbed.

The others immediately stopped shouting. Worry lined the facilitator's face. "You okay?"

Laura regained her composure and nodded. "I've heard screaming and confusion my whole life."

"Life is full of distractions," the facilitator agreed. "But David learned to follow God's lead rather than the noise around him."

"Can I try again?"

The second time through the minefield, the other voices lost their power because Laura focused on her coach. She pulled off her blindfold on the other side and beamed.

By the end of camp, Laura left a different person. Facing the different challenges gave her a new confidence. "I feel like I can endure anything."

Two Thumbs Up

Carol Joy, director of Hood River, Oregon, T.R.A.C., knew Kurt got angered easily. Her son had been in the same cabin with him at another summer camp and spent most of the time diffusing Kurt so he wouldn't punch things in his frustration.

At T.R.A.C., Carol Joy decided to pair Kurt with a counselor who worked for years with special needs kids in the school district. The match was perfect, and Kurt proved to be invaluable on the challenge course because of his height. Other than one small incident, Kurt never showed his anger.

By the end of camp, Kurt didn't want to leave. Carol Joy had a flashback to her son's camp when Kurt had stomped off and hid in the car while the other campers said goodbye. At T.R.A.C., though, he fit in with others who faced similar giants in their lives.

With much coaxing, Kurt boarded the bus. At the top step, he turned around and put his thumbs in the air. "This camp is two thumbs up."

2.2

Buc, one of the facilitators at Glendale, Arizona, T.R.A.C., handed each camper a piece of PVC pipe which had been cut in half lengthwise.

"What's this for?" one of the teens asked.

"To make a marble run." Buc held up a marble. "As a team, your challenge is to move this marble around the challenge course using the PVC pipe."

"Huh?" one of the boys grunted.

Buc overlapped two pieces to demonstrate. "Hold your pieces together to make a long trough. Once the marble passes out of your section, run to the other end. Link your pipe with the others so the marble can roll down a continuous moving path."

"What if the marble drops?"

"Avoid that." Buc grinned. "David had to face obstacles like lions and bears before he fought Goliath. Now it's your turn."

The boys extended their arms to join their pieces. After a bit of trial and error, the team clicked, and the marble rolled down the pipe without dropping, even when the campers skirted trees and climbed a hill.

During the debriefing session, Buc posed a question.

"So, what about your life? What obstacles have you had to face?"

"Moving," someone piped up.

"Getting held back a grade," another camper said.

"I was taken from my mom seven times," a big African-American kid named Jethro shared. "The last time, she committed suicide the next day."

Buc and the counselors tried to hide their shock. The facilitator stumbled through another question. "On a scale of 1 to 10, how much do you trust the others here?"

Jethro didn't hesitate. "2.2," he answered.

Buc nodded slowly. He'd never heard a number, much less a fraction, given so quickly.

Three days and several challenges later, the group stood in front of the "spider web."

"You need to work together so that each of you passes through the ropes," Buc explained. "No one can touch the ground, and every person has to go through a different hole." Doubt filled a few faces, but the group rose to the challenge. When the last camper made it through the ropes, a cheer rang out.

"Now what do you think?" asked Buc. "What's your trust level in your team today?"

Jethro was the first to answer. "2.2 billion."

Buc couldn't believe the change. "And what have you learned?"

"Put my faith in God." Jethro grinned. "And trust Him."

Conquering Goliath

Kevin's application raised some red flags, but Gary preferred to evaluate campers without relying on labels. As co-director and facilitator at Scio, Oregon, T.R.A.C., he was glad to leave those details to the behavior specialist and his wife, Palma.

During orientation, Gary observed a camper who hung back from the group. Long hair covered his eyes. While the others used stones to design a logo to represent their cabin groups, Kevin didn't engage.

That afternoon the same young man got frustrated at archery when Brad, one of the volunteers, tried to explain the proper shooting stance. Kevin threw down his bow and sulked a few feet away.

Brad waited for Kevin to cool off and then approached him. "Kevin, I want to apologize. I didn't mean to offend you. Can you forgive me?"

Surprise flickered in Kevin's eyes. "Okay."

"Want to try again?" Kevin agreed.

Later on the challenge course, Gary introduced the Nitro challenge. "God had to prepare David for battle against Goliath. So you, too, must ready yourselves." The boys eyed the dangling rope. "Your first test — retrieve the rope. Next — get every member from one platform to the other."

The athletic boys swung easily across, but Kevin lacked upper body strength.

"Come on," the group encouraged. "You can do it."

After the third attempt, someone made a suggestion. "What if we made a loop?"

The idea made all the difference. Kevin let out a war whoop on the other side.

The hardest challenge came the last day. Kevin stared up at the wall and protested, "I can't climb that."

Like before, the others strategically scaled the wall. Two counselors stayed behind to help Kevin. Balancing him on their knees with others pulling from above, they succeeded.

"I did it!" Kevin screamed at the top, and applause rang out. "I conquered Goliath."

Gary didn't want the last session to end any more than the boys. "How about one more challenge called Willow in the Wind?"

Kevin stepped forward with some hesitation after several others tried.

"Cross your arms, and close your eyes," Gary explained. "Then lean without bending your knees."

The boys formed a tight circle around Kevin. They extended their hands and gently pushed Kevin as he fell in their direction.

"This is awesome." Kevin bobbed around the circle. "I feel like I'm floating."

Just Three Days

When the motion stopped, Kevin opened his eyes. A grin spread from ear to ear. "I never would've done that the first day. I didn't trust anyone."

Three days makes a difference.

Where's Jimmy?

"I hate this group," Jimmy scowled after the group disbanded from Cross Talk.

Tim, director of Omaha, Nebraska, T.R.A.C., stepped in to talk with the athletic black teenager. Jimmy wanted to be in another group with a friend, but the pair had caused too much trouble the year before.

"I don't like the rules." He crossed his arms.

Tim tried to reason with the teen. "Life is about rules."

"I know people who don't follow rules," Jimmy argued.

Tim wasn't going to debate the issue. "I got all day to sit with you."

Jimmy slumped down. A fish broke the surface of the lake. A water trampoline promised fun.

Tim finally spoke up. "What's really going on, Jimmy?"

"Why do we have to make a stop in Lincoln to pick up campers?" Tears filled his eyes. "My mom's there, and I want to see her."

Tim listened to the giants this young man faced. When the emotions were spent, Tim asked Jimmy if he was ready to join his group again.

He shook his head.

The radio suddenly crackled with Jeff's voice. "Anybody seen Jimmy?" the facilitator asked. "We really need him at the wall."

The camper lit up. "Maybe I better go."

Later, Jeff told Tim that Jimmy opened up on the challenge course for the first time.

Tim smiled. Sometimes it was just nice knowing you were missed.

Part One: David and Goliath

Dear T.R.A.C. Staff,

Just a note to say thank you for a wonderful time at camp and for allowing me the opportunity to come. My favorite part of camp was archery ... I actually got a bull's-eye! Fishing and horseback riding were a great time, too, and I caught two fish. The first fish jumped off my hook, but I got the second one. The food was great, and so were the people in the activity center. They took time to help me do my project and didn't get impatient with me. I will always have great memories of camp ... thank you for giving them to me.

Love and smiles!
Henry

A Challenge

A cheer rang out as the last girl was lifted into the air by the group at the challenge course. Clouds streaked the blue sky above at Kitsap County, Washington, T.R.A.C.

"Do you think you can lift me?" Mark asked. At 6 feet, 3 inches and 240-plus pounds, the facilitator was twice the size of most of the girls.

They immediately rose to the challenge. Working together had given the girls new confidence, and they faced the giant of failure head-on.

Mark lay down on the ground, while Scott, the director, spotted his head. The girls surrounded Mark and positioned their hands.

"One, two, three," they called out in unison.

Slowly, Mark rose. The girls lifted him into the air. Both Mark and Scott couldn't believe it. The girls did it!

Addiction

Matthew came to camp after another camper backed out and a spot opened.

The application said Matthew was 15. In reality, he was two years older.

Dan, co-director of Sherwood, Oregon, T.R.A.C., stepped in when cigarettes were found in Matthew's bag.

"They're mine," Matthew protested. "You can't take them."

"You can't have the cigarettes," Dan explained. "It's not safe because it's too dry out here. The camp could burn."

"Then I'm leaving."

Dan's voice rose with impatience. He was scheduled to meet back at the conference room with the new directors-in-training, and he wasn't getting through to Matthew. "You can't have the cigarettes, Matthew. But we want you at camp."

"It doesn't sound like it," Matthew muttered.

Dan exhaled. He knew he'd blown it when he raised his voice. "I'm sorry, Matthew. I didn't mean to yell at you."

Matthew shrugged. "It's alright. Everyone else does."

"No, it's wrong, Matthew," Dan persisted. "And I'm sorry."

Matthew agreed to stay. During Cross Talk, he impressed his counselor, Jim, with his understanding of the Bible. He even confided his fear about starting a new high school.

"Kids can size you up immediately," Jim advised Matthew. "In seconds, they'll push your buttons, and you'll be the one getting suspended."

Later, at the awards ceremony, Dan gave Matthew a perseverance bead. Matthew had an addiction, and Dan wished he'd been more sensitive. Three days must've felt like a lifetime to the young smoker. "Thanks for sticking it out, Matthew. I'm so glad you were at camp."

The following year, Jim ran into Matthew. "Guess what?" Matthew smiled. "I didn't get kicked out of school."

Jim congratulated Matthew. He'd slain the giant of defeat and persevered — just like he'd been challenged to do at T.R.A.C.

Simple Things

The girls clambered to be heard over one another. Each had a different solution for the teepee shuffle. In the challenge, the girls had to rearrange themselves on a long pole without falling off.

Terresa, helping with both Cross Talk and the challenge course her first year at the Scio, Oregon, camp, listened without commenting. Teegan, a tiny girl not more than 5 feet tall, had a suggestion, but no one heard. At 14, the quiet girl screamed for attention through her actions — not her words. She was a cutter and a prostitute. Teegan supported her meth habit by turning tricks.

When the group exhausted their ideas without success, Terresa nudged Teegan to give her solution. Within minutes, the girls accomplished the challenge. Pride shined on their faces.

"What would you have missed if you hadn't listened to Teegan?" Terresa asked them.

"We would've failed," someone piped up.

"Why was it so hard to hear her?" Terresa made them think.

"Other people are louder and more confident. It was easier to believe them."

The Nitro challenge came the following day. The girls had to cross from one platform to another using a long rope dangling from a tree. This time, the girls were quick to listen to everyone, and they accomplished the challenge faster together.

"What was different today?" Terresa asked them.

"Encouragement," a camper answered.

Simple things, really. Like the stones David used to slay Goliath.

Someone to listen.

Someone to encourage.

Someone to show girls like Teegan life can be different.

Scars

"Wanna paddleboat with me?" Devon asked Cindy, director of The Woodlands, Texas, T.R.A.C.

"Sure." She put on a lifejacket and joined the tall kid with bad acne. Water lapped against the sides of their boat.

"There was a brown recluse spider crawling around," Devon told Cindy. "But don't worry. I got rid of it for you."

Nervous laughter escaped Cindy's lips. "Thanks."

"You don't want to get bit by one of those."

"No, I don't," Cindy quickly agreed.

"I got bit once."

"No!" Cindy exclaimed.

"Right here." Devon showed Cindy a hole on his knee where skin was missing.

"That's awful."

"Yeah, it was pretty nasty."

"What happened to your other knee?" Cindy pointed to another scar.

"Oh, that's where I got shot."

"You were shot?" Cindy tried not to show her surprise.

"Yeah, I was 4 years old. My dad was doing drugs and

got in trouble with some gangs. They came by and shot through our house. And I got shot. That was the last time I saw my dad."

Cindy looked closer at the boy and saw the visible marks which marred his body. *What scars couldn't she see?*

One of the counselors, a teacher and long-time summer camp counselor, remarked on the genuine gratitude she saw in the teens at T.R.A.C. For kids like Devon, camp isn't one more thing to fill up long summer days, like sports camps, educational programs or art and music lessons. Camp is a reprieve from fighting giants.

Part One: David and Goliath

Often times people call me Eeyore ... Going into camp, that was a great concern for me ... I prayed that the Lord would give me the energy and attitude that I would need to really connect with the kids.

Well, wouldn't ya know it, my prayer was answered! The minute those kids got off the bus, I could just see the hurt in their faces, and I instantly became a totally different person ... I found myself being challenged, stretched, forced to trust, crying, laughing, frustrated, screaming, totally exhausted, joyous and more ... I saw kids smiling, laughing, screaming, singing, praying, listening, getting hugs, giving hugs, running away, running back, crying ... many who didn't even want to get off the bus when they arrived (were) crying when the bus came to pick them up.

Going into camp, my faith and walk in Christ had really become stagnant. I had lost focus on the Lord and His word while being caught up in the hustle and bustle of the worldly life ... Spending time with the kids has helped me to realize how much I have been missing the Lord Jesus Christ and His word in my daily life ... I am very thankful to the Lord for placing me at T.R.A.C.

Corey, first-time T.R.A.C. volunteer

Music Chick

René stood behind her keyboard on the wooden stage at Hood River, Oregon, T.R.A.C. Insecurities she battled in junior high reared up like giants as she stared across her audience of teen boys sitting on hay bales. *What was she thinking? She was a backup musician, not a solo act. Definitely not music director.*

After worship and Cross Talk, René milled around with the campers.

"Hey, you're pretty good," one of the boys complimented her.

Another agreed. "Yeah, we should call you 'Music Chick.'"

René couldn't hide her smile. "Music Chick" stuck.

The following year, René felt more comfortable in her role. The nickname took the pressure off being music director. She connected with the returning campers and felt God explode her heart for this awkward age.

At girls' camp, Tasha and Melanie jumped up on stage. "Can we sing with you?"

René pounded out the chords to "How Great is Our God," and the rest of the girls joined in.

Part One: David and Goliath

The scent of pine filled the air as René looked toward a cloudless blue sky. The "Music Chick" sang her heart out with the girls.

Dropping the Ball

"I dropped the ball with Kyla," Jeff confided in Tim, director of Omaha, Nebraska, T.R.A.C. "I let Kyla down. I just wasn't relating to her."

Tim tried to encourage the facilitator who had such a heart for the teens at camp. Kyla wasn't an active girl; she didn't say much, so it was difficult to know what she thought of camp.

The next day, Tim joined a group hiking to the rope bridge.

"Think you'll get wet?" Tim asked the girls. The bridge crossed to an island, dipping close to the water. Enough weight meant wet shoes and fun.

Everyone was excited, except for Kyla. She waited to cross last and froze in the middle. "I can't do this."

"Yes, you can, Kyla," Tim encouraged her. "You can do this."

Kyla took a tentative step. The bridge swayed, and she gripped the sides.

"Come on, Kyla. You can make it," the girls cheered from the island.

Kyla took a deep breath and walked the last few steps.

Part One: David and Goliath

The girls erupted in excitement. They surrounded Kyla with hugs and high fives. A huge smile crossed her face.

"I knew you could do it," Tim said. "You faced your fears and did it. Great job."

Camp ended, and Tim called Kyla's foster mom in January to invite Kyla to a bowling party for campers.

"I don't know what happened at that camp this summer," the foster mom exclaimed.

"Oh, yeah?" Tim took a deep breath, expecting the worst. "What do you mean?"

"Kyla came home changed. Not just for a day. Or a month. She changed permanently — her attitude, her confidence, everything."

Joy bubbled inside Tim as he remembered Kyla facing her giant of fear at the rope bridge.

"In fact," the foster mom continued, "Kyla changed so much, we adopted her."

Jeff's words reverberated in Tim's head. *I dropped the ball with Kyla.*

Tim hung up the phone, dumbfounded. Jeff was never holding the ball. God was. And He had plans all along for Kyla at camp.

The Wall

Pablo gazed up at the 12-foot wall the boys nicknamed "Goliath."

"Come on, Pablo. You can do it," one of the other T.R.A.C. campers called out.

Being out in the middle of the Kansas Flint Hills was a stretch for the overweight teenager who preferred video games to the outdoors. In his 14 years, he'd lived in 12 foster homes.

Scaling the wall appeared impossible.

"Yeah, man. We'll help you."

Pablo attempted to jump, but only gained six inches. "This is stupid!" he growled.

"Dude, we believe in you," another camper called out. The group gathered around him, and the encouragement grew.

Pablo sighed. He didn't want to disappoint his new friends, but the giant of failure taunted him. "Okay," he finally agreed.

Grunting and groaning, Pablo strained while all of the campers and counselors worked together to help him over the wall.

The effort paid off. Pablo made it to the top.

Part One: David and Goliath

The team erupted in cheers.

"I did it!" Pablo screamed, grabbing the staff at the top of the wall in huge bear hugs. "I beat Goliath! Thank you."

A proud Pablo scrawled his autograph among the other names on the wall.

Zip Line

It didn't take Amy long to find Will, co-director of Kearney, Nebraska, T.R.A.C., after she alighted off the bus at camp.

"The picture you painted for me last year is next to our family computer." Will referred to the miniature canvas Amy had painted of the camp's tower and zip line.

The olive-skinned girl with braces and dark hair grinned from ear to ear.

"Are you going to face your giant and go down the zip line this year?"

Dark eyes shined with admiration. Amy's attachment to Will and the male facilitators at camp came from her deep longing for a father in her life. "I'm going to try."

"I'll be there," Will promised.

On Sunday, Amy had reservations. She looked up at the 42-foot tower and wavered.

"Maybe next year."

Will hesitated, thinking of his job with the National Guard. "I'm being deployed next year."

Amy's face dropped. She'd been to the Kearney camp since it had started three years earlier. "Really?"

Will nodded.

Part One: David and Goliath

Amy grabbed the harness with resolve, tightened the straps and climbed the stairs. Minutes ticked by as she sat on the edge of the tower, her harness attached to the steel cable by carabineer clips. Fluffy white clouds drifted lazily in a baby blue sky.

"You can do it," Will encouraged Amy, his own harness also attached to the zip line.

Below, campers and staff echoed their support. "You can do it, Amy!"

She shook her head. "I can't." Amy pushed herself up to a standing position and walked back down the flight of stairs.

Will couldn't convince her to try again, so he left to take care of final camp details. Not long after, a call came over the radio. Amy was ready to try again.

Back in his harness, Will climbed the tower and found Amy sitting on the edge, fear evident in her wide eyes.

"Let's do a countdown," Will suggested.

"Ten, nine, eight ..."

Amy didn't move.

Campers shouted their encouragement from below. Will started multiple countdowns, trying every angle to convince Amy to beat her giant.

Finally, after 45 minutes, Amy pushed off the edge. The whir of the wire rang through the air. Will hurried to follow on the second zip line. Campers and staff screamed in delight.

"You did it!" Will gave Amy a side hug back on the ground.

A shaky Amy couldn't stop grinning.

They started walking toward the other campers, and Will collapsed on the ground, overcome with emotion.

A speechless young lady watched tears trickle down Will's face. After three years, Amy had conquered her giant and touched a soldier's heart.

Part One: David and Goliath

Dear T.R.A.C. Staff,

I loved camp! I'm glad I had a chance to go for three years. It seems to me that every year gets more and more exciting. This is one of my favorite camps because you don't just go to have fun — you also learn.

I think my favorite part of camp is the horseback riding. The first year I was scared to ride, but once I did, I fell in love with riding. This year's challenge course was more intense, and it encouraged me to want to be a part of it all. It was amazing how teamwork could make so much happen. The nature hike was peaceful, and I loved getting my first bull's-eye at archery.

Thank you for everything. You guys are all so nice to take your time to make it all possible for foster kids to go to camp. I love going to camp!

Reagan

Writing on the Rocks

Terresa asked James and Brad to join her on stage for Cross Talk at Scio, Oregon, T.R.A.C. She turned to James. "You're what? Five-foot-two?"

The camper nodded.

"You're going to be David."

Brad smiled, anticipating his role. The archery volunteer dwarfed James at more than 6 feet, 5 inches and 250 pounds.

Terresa turned to her audience. "Add the stage to Brad's height, and you got Goliath." She pointed to a wooden shield with straps. "Saul gave David his shield to fight Goliath, so, James, see if you can pick that up."

James eyed the added weights.

"It's roughly equal to Goliath's armor."

James struggled to pick up the shield. "Dang! That's heavy."

Brad stepped in to help, and the two carried it across the stage.

"How do you think God feels when we carry our weights?" Terresa asked.

"He helped me." James pointed to Brad. "Just like my friends."

Terresa nodded. "But how far did you both carry the shield before you had to drop it?"

"Three feet."

Terresa looked over the group. "We pick up our pain and our shame. But God wants us to put our weights at His feet and walk away."

Thoughtful silence filled the crowd.

Terresa passed out Sharpie markers. "Take one of the rocks on stage and write down the thing in your life which hurts the most."

When the last camper finished, the group headed to the creek. "Toss off your burdens." Terresa threw the rock in her hand. "Let God take what you're carrying."

Emotion charged the air. One boy after another lobbed his rock into the current.

Later, Terresa and Palma noticed several rocks near the mouth of the swimming hole when they cleaned up after camp. Terresa saw the Sharpie writing. "Look. The water carried the boys' rocks downstream."

She lifted one out of the water and read, "Anger."

Palma read another. "Shame."

Water tumbled over the face of other rocks, rippling the letters on more words.

"Abandonment."

"Not loved."

"Not good enough."

The women held the rocks close to their hearts and breathed a prayer for each of the boys.

Part Two
Illuminating Our Lives with Truth:
The Story of Joseph

Many first-time campers at T.R.A.C. mask their nervousness with indifference or defiance. Familiar with rejection, teens in foster care build walls to protect their hearts. Questions plague them as they struggle with issues of identity. *Why did my father leave me and my siblings? Why didn't Mom protect me from her boyfriend? Why did my parents abandon me?*

Joseph is the Biblical character highlighted during the second year of Cross Talk. Thrown into a pit and sold into slavery by his brothers, Joseph knew the pain of rejection and betrayal. He found refuge in an Egyptian official's house, only to meet with trouble. Falsely accused and imprisoned, Joseph's story could have ended without hope. But God was with Joseph — even in the darkness. He used Joseph to interpret the dreams of Pharaoh and saved Egypt and Israel from seven years of famine.

Campers easily relate to injustice. Judges and caseworkers make decisions with little input from the lives impacted. Teens in foster care often suffer for years until they find a house to call home. Some age out of the system before knowing love and acceptance.

Many campers across the country are finding hope at T.R.A.C. They identify with Joseph and begin to see God has not forgotten them. They memorize Psalm 139:12, which reads, "Even the darkness will not be dark to you; the night will shine like the day, for darkness is as light to you."

Just as Joseph forgave his brothers, campers are challenged to find freedom in forgiveness so that what was intended to harm, God can make good.

Lili's Camp

Serena pulled her coat around her swollen belly and stepped outside the emergency room. Her breath immediately condensed in a cloud. Tim's chest pains had been a scare, and she was still shaky. The baby was due in two months. Serena couldn't imagine raising an infant and a toddler without her husband. He was only 36. *What if things had turned out differently? What if he'd had a heart attack rather than esophageal flu?*

"Hey, lady," a voice interrupted Serena's troubled thoughts. "Can you help us?"

Two boys huddled over a pair of puppies.

"What's wrong?" Serena bent down to examine the dogs.

"This one won't eat," the bigger boy said. "We think the mama abandoned them with all the recent flooding."

Serena's eyes filled with tears. "What have you been feeding them?"

"Free samples from Petco. We used water to soften the food."

Serena took the sickly dog in her arms. The dog's coloring looked like a German shepherd, with a mix of Rottweiler.

"Hey, pup." She touched the small head. "I'll be right back."

Soon two nurses joined her outside. The puppy lapped at a syringe filled with sugar water.

"Look at that." The boys grinned. "She likes it."

Serena smiled. "Keep using the syringe, and she'll gain back her strength."

The bigger boy shuffled his feet. "We can't keep dogs at the shelter. Will you take her?"

Serena's heart melted. "I have to ask my husband." She nestled the pup inside her coat and walked into the emergency room. Serena already had a name picked out.

"Miss, miss!" A security guard who'd been observing their group called out.

Serena winced, but didn't turn around. Her shoes clicked faster against the linoleum floor.

"Miss, miss!" He caught up with her. "You can't bring a dog in here."

"She's gonna die." Serena showed him the puppy's sweet face. "Please, can I talk to my husband?"

The guard hesitated, but relented. "Make it quick."

Serena ducked into the hospital room and saw her heavily medicated husband. He looked pale against the hospital sheets. "Can we keep Lili?"

Tim's grunt was all the affirmation Serena needed. Lili became a member of the family.

Years later, a healthy Lili romped on Tim and Serena's property in Sherwood, Oregon. A group of campers tossed a Frisbee back and forth in a game of keep away from Lili.

Serena sat on the porch, watching the game, when one of the boys, a quiet kid with sandy brown hair, joined her.

"I think you named the camp wrong." Wesley looked at her with bright blue eyes.

"Oh, yeah?" Her eyebrows lifted. "What do you want to name it?"

"Lili's Camp." He smiled. "Lili thinks we come to camp to see her."

They both laughed as Lili snatched the Frisbee and took off. The boys dashed after her.

Wesley was right. Lili followed campers to the fishing hole and even let the girls dress her in feather boas. She brought many smiles to those in circumstances similar to the boys who rescued her. Maybe Lili loved teens at T.R.A.C. because she knew what it meant to be abandoned. Lili loved because love transformed her.

Just Three Days

Dear God,

Thank You so much for everything You have done for me, because without You I would be nothing. Thank You for this wonderful heart-touching, life-saving camp. I have learned so much; it's hard to forgive sometimes and coming here really makes it a little bit easier.

Joan

Bad Kid?

Laughter bounced around the blue cabin at Kearney, Nebraska, T.R.A.C. as the subject turned to female anatomy. Before the counselors could intervene, 12-year-old A.J. piped up. "Hey, guys, we shouldn't be talking about breasts."

The boys responded to the likeable teen with ebony skin and changed subjects. Ryan, one of the counselors in the group, was impressed. Only recently had he committed his own life to Christ; at A.J.'s age, he'd been more interested in smoking and drinking.

Later that night, A.J. sat in rapt attention as Keith Becker, the speaker from the Todd Becker Foundation, told the boys how his brother had been killed his senior year of high school in an alcohol-related car wreck because of his party lifestyle. Keith related how choices to view pornography in his brother's freshmen year led him down the wide path of destruction.

After a campfire and s'mores, A.J. returned to the cabin and crawled into his bunk. Under the covers of his sleeping bag, he turned on his flashlight and began reading the new teen Bible he'd received at Cross Talk. Ryan observed A.J. from across the log cabin.

The next morning a look of concern filled A.J.'s face. "Is it really true we have to gouge out our eyes if we look at a woman lustfully?"

Ryan and the other counselors chuckled. "No." They shook their heads. "We just need to look at women as children of God. Not sexual objects."

Relief flooded A.J.'s face.

After a day filled with paintball, archery, fishing, swimming, the challenge course and zip line, A.J. read the story of Joseph out loud with the others in his cabin. The counselors' deep voices mixed with the younger voices which occasionally cracked from adolescence.

Cross Talk on Sunday focused on forgiveness. Bob, the teacher, encouraged the campers to forgive those who'd wronged them just like Joseph forgave his brothers. While "I Forgive You" by Kris Strobeck played, the campers wrote a letter expressing their inner thoughts.

"Dear T.R.A.C.," A.J. wrote, "I'm confessing I am a bad kid. I used to be a pervert and cursed a lot, but as I came to this camp, I believe I've changed. I'm learning more about God, and I want this to happen. Thank you, T.R.A.C., for everything. It was fun, and I learned new things. I'd love to stay longer. God bless you all."

At lunch, Ryan noticed the distress on A.J.'s face.

"You okay, man?"

A tear streaked his dark skin.

"Let's go outside. Get some fresh air." Ryan asked Gail, one of the facilitators, to accompany them out of the dining room.

Part Two: The Story of Joseph

The trio sat on a bench. Potted impatiens splashed color around them.

"I don't want to be a bad person anymore," A.J. confessed.

Gail and Ryan talked about walking the narrow road mentioned by the speaker on Friday night.

"I want to be a Christian." A.J. bowed his head and asked Jesus to be Lord of his life. A beaming young man walked back into the dining room. Ryan raised his voice to announce A.J.'s decision, and the crowd erupted.

Guilt no longer weighing him down, the "bad kid" found hope at T.R.A.C. and freedom in forgiveness.

Hope

"Life can break us." Candi, art teacher at Ventura, California, T.R.A.C., paused. The girls seated around the multi-purpose room could all relate. One had delivered a baby at age 11. Another spent days in a closet. Each had a story.

"Life broke Joseph. He was thrown in a pit and sold into slavery by his own brothers." Her eyes locked onto several campers. "Sometimes it's the very people we love who break us the most."

Candi picked up a terra cotta pot and placed it inside a brown paper lunch bag. "You have a pot in front of you which you can smash with a hammer." Several eyebrows arched. "Imagine you are the pot. How broken are you?"

Giggles peppered the sound of terra cotta breaking. Some were cautious. Others pounded with reckless abandon. As the last whack died, Candi invited the girls to re-glue their pots in some fashion.

Brown bags crinkled as campers spilled the fragments onto paper plates. Those who tried rebuilding their pots to the original shape realized their folly. A few pushed back their chairs and quit. Others persevered and used tissue paper, glitter glue and confetti to create new masterpieces.

Part Two: The Story of Joseph

Even those who'd given up eventually tried again and became engrossed in recreating something new.

Beauty soon emerged. Jani glued the word "life" onto a fragment and scrambled the letters "i, e, l and f" underneath. "I mixed up the letters because sometimes life gets all scrambled up," the camper said, explaining her creation to Candi's helper, Lynne.

"Can you tell me about this?" she asked Jani, pointing to a large terra cotta piece on top. As the founding art teacher at Ventura T.R.A.C., Lynne wanted craft time to be more meaningful by using art to help heal and transform.

"That's all the bad stuff that happens in life," Jani answered without hesitation. "But no matter how dark it seems, there is always light shining through."

"Can we throw away the broken pieces we don't want?" two girls wanted to know.

"If you'd like." Candi nodded. "Or you could be more purposeful and glue those pieces onto another plate."

A camper named DeDe made a sad face with the discarded pieces. "That represents the bad things I want to leave behind." She smiled as she turned to her new creation. "And this represents my life flowering before me."

Color.

Texture.

Beauty.

Hope emerged from the rubble as each girl began to see past the brokenness and believe in the possibilities.

A Symbol

Fireworks exploded above the creek at Scio, Oregon, sparking excitement in the T.R.A.C. campers. Laughter filled the summer night.

"Can you quit?" Scotty asked a kid who was whistling.

"He's just happy." Ted, Scotty's counselor, tried to diffuse the situation. "Don't let it bug you."

The young man stopped, but then forgot and let loose again.

Scotty bolted, so Ted had to call for help.

After Scotty talked with the behavior specialist and Palma, the director, Ted found Scotty in the cabin on the top bunk. His whole body was rigid.

Night brought terror for Scotty. He hadn't slept the night before, so Palma gave Ted a wooden cross for Scotty. One side read, "Jesus." The other read, "Peace."

"I'm scared," Scotty confided. "When I close my eyes, I hear people wailing and screaming."

Ted thought of hell.

"Even if I sleep, bad dreams haunt me." Scotty told Ted how his stepdad had abused him.

No wonder the nightmare was so real; Scotty had lived his own private hell.

Part Two: The Story of Joseph

"Take this." Ted handed Scotty the cross, wondering if something so simple could make an impact. "It's a symbol to help remind you God is here."

Scotty clung to the cross and laid his head on his pillow.

"Dear God," Ted prayed. "Please deliver Scotty from this recurring dream and give him real rest." Before the last words ended, Scotty drifted off. He slept the entire night in a deep sleep.

The cross was enough. Like Psalm 139:12 tells us, "Even the darkness will not be dark to you; the night will shine like the day, for darkness is as light to you."

Jesus alone would help Scotty conquer the nightmare.

Bible Burning?

Sunlight blanketed the outdoor pavilion at Kearney, Nebraska, T.R.A.C., promising an afternoon of fun at the waterfront.

"I don't believe in God." Josiah's eyes flashed as he and his counselor, Kelvin, talked after Cross Talk.

Kelvin looked up from reading about Joseph and forgiveness in the camper journal.

"I want to burn the Bible," Josiah hissed. "It's nothing more than a bunch of science fiction."

Kelvin looked at Josiah over the rims of his reading glasses, compassion stirring inside him for the camper. He said nothing, only listened. He knew little about Josiah, except that the young man had been in his current foster home for six months. *What had caused the 13 year old to form such a strong opinion?*

Later, Josiah noticed a reference to Romans 8:13 etched on his bunk. "What's this?"

"A verse in the Bible," Kelvin answered.

Josiah gave a half-smirk, surprised at the scriptural graffiti. Soon the camper opened his new Bible and read out loud, "For if you live according to the sinful nature, you will die; but if by the Spirit you put to death the misdeeds of the body, you will live."

"That's a good verse," Kelvin commented.

Josiah nodded.

On Sunday, Josiah volunteered to pray for the last meal at camp. On the bus ride home, he surprised Kelvin by reading his Bible for more than 30 minutes.

Three days can challenge the biggest skeptic and point him to the truth.

Letter to God

Kathie pointed to the easel on the Cross Talk stage at Sherwood, Oregon, T.R.A.C. "We've been talking about Joseph and forgiveness," she told the boys. "So if anyone wants to write on this whiteboard, this is like a letter to God."

No one moved.

Mike, one of the counselors, finally broke the silence. "I need to forgive my father." As he made his way forward, the boys were visibly impressed by the vulnerability of a man in his 50s writing to God.

Kathie hid her shock when a camper named Darrol stepped up next. His rage made him unstable, so the staff had been monitoring him carefully throughout camp.

"I need to forgive my dad." Darrol swore. "If God can forgive me, than he can forgive my dad."

Darrol took a seat, and sobs racked his body. His counselor put an arm around his shoulders.

More campers stepped forward.

I need to forgive my mom …

I need to forgive my dad …

Names filled the whiteboard as one camper after another poured out his heart in a letter to God.

Adrian's Rock

"This is for you." Adrian handed a rock to Michael, his "big camper" (counselor) from Royal Family KIDS in Glendale, Arizona.

"I wrote my name on it." The boy squeezed his arms around Michael. "That way you won't forget me."

Michael swallowed the lump that lodged in his throat. The boy with endless energy had stolen his heart.

I'm not going to do this again, Michael told himself. He couldn't listen to one more 11 year old ask, "What about next year? Is there a camp for teens?"

He pocketed Adrian's rock, vowing to do something.

The next day, Michael and his friend Kelli co-founded a non-profit Christian organization in Arizona called Hope & A Future (www.azhope.com). Like Michael, foster kids had captured Kelli's heart. Volunteering with Royal Family KIDS had prompted her to teach art at a group home.

Michael discovered Teen Reach Adventure Camp when he searched online.

The timing was perfect. Directors' training began the following week, so Kelli boarded a plane for Oregon, and

Just Three Days

Arizona hosted its first T.R.A.C. the next summer of 2006.

Adrian's rock sits atop Michael's desk. The boy didn't attend T.R.A.C. because like many, he got lost in the system. Michael didn't forget Adrian. He remembers the skinny kid with the beaming smile and buzzed brown hair and presses on to serve other Adrians who feel left in the pit — abandoned and forgotten.

Volunteers Needed

Debbie, director of Ventura, California, T.R.A.C., stared at the long list of names on the waiting list. Her heart broke for the girls who wouldn't get to come to camp.

Out of the blue, the phone rang. A nearby church heard about T.R.A.C. and wanted to hear more about ministering to teens in foster care. A few weeks later, Debbie spoke in front of the congregation. The response was huge. Because of the volunteers who signed up, nearly every camper on the waiting list enjoyed camp.

Today T.R.A.C. directors across the country are praying for volunteers to step forward. One counselor means two teens can attend camp — teens who otherwise feel stuck in a pit, like Joseph, with no way out.

Three days is a small investment with eternal results. As one person noted, "To the world, you may be one person, but to one person, you may be the world."

Forgiveness

"Camden isn't coming to camp," the boy's mother told Angela, co-director of Kearney, Nebraska, T.R.A.C., three days before registration. "He wants to make money detasseling corn."

"Can he take a break for the weekend?" Angela tried to hide her frustration. Volunteers and donors gave generously of their time and money so 32 boys could attend T.R.A.C.; she hated to see one spot empty.

"Nope." The woman refused to budge. "Thanks, anyway."

Angela glanced at her list of campers. Her eyes fell on a young man living with a great foster family who often took teens in transition.

"Hey, Tina," Angela greeted the foster mom over the phone. "We're excited to see Mark in a few days. Any chance you know of another boy who might like to come to T.R.A.C.? We just had an opening."

"Really?" Tina got excited. "Jeremy's been in our home for a few days while he's in transition. Camp would be great for him. His adoption just failed."

Angela choked back her emotions. Many on their team prayed God would fill camp with the teens He wanted to touch; obviously God didn't want any vacancies, either.

"Any issues I should know about?"

"He has R.A.D., Reactive Attachment Disorder."

Angela nodded, knowing the many challenges that came because a child never bonded with a caregiver in his formative years. Trust issues were huge. Animal cruelty was another concern Tina had.

"When Jeremy came to our house, though," Tina continued, "his first question was, 'Do you guys go to church here'?"

Friday morning, a crowd of excited counselors and staff stood under a grove of evergreens. Music blared as they waved signs to welcome campers who disembarked from the bus. Jeremy searched the faces to find his name. His eyes landed on a colorful poster held by a familiar face.

"Nathan?" Jeremy squeaked.

Nathan grinned from ear to ear. He'd been Jeremy's "big camper" (counselor) several years earlier at Royal Family KIDS Camp. "Hey, Jeremy."

Jeremy embraced his counselor. "I never thought I'd see you again."

Jeremy volunteered for the first mealtime prayer at camp. A likeable kid, he wanted to try everything and formed a strong bond with Nathan. Except for picking on the llamas and goats near the horse-riding venue, Jeremy was an ideal camper.

Just Three Days

When Bob, the Cross Talk teacher, talked about Joseph forgiving his brothers and our need to forgive those who've hurt us, Jeremy responded with the following letter:

> Thank you, T.R.A.C., for letting me learn to forgive. I didn't trust anybody. I especially love you as a best friend, Nathan. Thanks for not letting me down. I'll miss you so much. I love this place. I trust you, Nathan.
>
> Thanks, Jeremy

Forgiveness can melt the hardest heart. God is bigger than any disorder.

The Nap

"Do you want to rest?" Carol Joy, director of Hood River, Oregon, T.R.A.C., asked Mitch on Saturday afternoon. He seemed wiped out compared to the other campers.

Mitch readily agreed, so she put on some restful music, and he slept soundly for several hours. Carol Joy thought nothing of Mitch's fatigue until she met Mitch's grandmother after camp.

"Thank you so much for sharing this." The older woman pointed to Mitch's camp memory album filled with pictures and positive I-Spys. "I'm so glad he did well for you because when I dropped him off, his medicine for his behavior rolled under the seat."

Her next words floored Carol Joy.

"Mitch's father died last week."

Carol Joy hid her shock until debriefing. Mitch lost his mother earlier in his life, and now his father had died. *What normal family would send a grieving teen to camp?* Then again — what was normal to most T.R.A.C. campers?

The following year, Mitch returned to camp with a

Goth look. The teen who seemed so out of place with his all-black clothes, black eyeliner and black nail polish thrived at the 120-acre camp in the Hood River Valley shadowed by Mt. Hood. Campers saw deer and elk, and staff chased black bears from the garbage.

During the closing ceremony, Mitch pushed back the graduation bead, knowing acceptance meant he couldn't return to camp. Mitch was adamant about returning to T.R.A.C. a third year. His birthday fell days after camp, so he could squeeze in one last camp before he turned 16.

The final year, the Goth look was gone. Carol Joy returned Mitch to the foster home where he'd lived since his grandmother could no longer care for him.

The closer they got to Portland, the more Mitch shut down. Carol Joy had seen it before in other campers. Reality stifled the boyhood delight experienced at camp.

"Can I come back again, please?" he pleaded.

This was the part Carol Joy hated. *What could she say?*

"You don't know what it's really like," Mitch confided. "How life is for me."

Hot tears burned Carol Joy's eyes. So many kids slipped through the cracks. Many times she wondered if the foster system should be abandoned altogether and kids placed once again in orphanages.

"Look us up in a few years." Carol Joy managed a smile. "Lord willing, we'll still be running camps."

Hope flickered in Mitch's eyes, reminding Carol Joy of her husband, who'd also been orphaned. At 16, his father died of a heart attack; at 17, his mother died in a car accident. God bred compassion through the pain, and David started T.R.A.C. on their property to help the orphaned.

"Please help Mitch know You're near." Carol Joy breathed a prayer for the boy who'd stolen her heart. Trusting was the hardest part of letting go, yet, like with Joseph, God could make good come from what was intended for harm.

Family

When pushed from one home to the next, foster teens identify with Joseph's rejection from his family. Foster teens grow up wondering what a family looks like. They ache to belong.

Carmen from Omaha, Nebraska, told one of the T.R.A.C. staff, "Every time I go to a new foster family, they want me to know how to act. But how can I know if I never get the chance to be part of a family?"

Tree Stump

"I was angry for a long time," one of the facilitators at The Woodlands, Texas, T.R.A.C. shared with a group of boys on the challenge course. The campers listened with rapt attention.

"I had lots of reasons to be mad. A history of neglect, a crummy family life, you name it." She looked each boy in the eye. "But finally, the weight got too heavy. I didn't want to carry it anymore."

Understanding sparked in several of the boys.

"You know what I mean, don't you?"

Heads bobbed in agreement. Like Joseph, many knew betrayal.

The facilitator picked up a rock. "This represents my anger when I finally gave it to God." She hurled it in the lake, and the splash echoed through the air. "When I finally let go, I felt free for the first time in my life." She paused. "You can do the same thing, if you want. Give God your anger."

Boys hurried to grab rocks. One after the other, they threw them into the lake. The rocks got bigger as each boy wanted to prove the enormity of his anger.

Jacob, an energetic teen with a great smile, searched

for the right rock. His eyes landed on a dead tree stump, too heavy to lift. Jacob wasn't deterred. He dragged it toward the lake, muscles straining.

The others stopped to watch him. "My anger's huge," he groaned.

Ragged breaths filled the silence. "I'm so mad at my mother." Jacob curled his fist when he dropped the stump at the water's edge. "When C.P.S. (Child Protective Services) came to pick me up, my mom didn't do anything. She just sat there and let them take me away."

He pushed the tree stump into the lake and choked up. Soon, sobs racked his body.

Campers and staff surrounded Jacob, pouring out words of comfort and affirmation.

A year later, Jacob returned to camp, excited to be partnered with a mentor through **T.R.A.C.**_life_.

"I've been reading my Bible every day," Jacob told Cindy, the director.

"That's great, Jacob." Cindy gave him a side hug. Jacob had warmed his way into her heart the first year she'd met him at Royal Family KIDS Camp.

"Camp is really special," he continued. "But I have a problem with one thing."

"Oh, yeah?" Cindy raised her eyebrows. "What's that?"

"It's way too short."

Different Planet

"People ask me all the time about my job at the youth treatment center," Lisa, the behavior specialist, confided in Angela, co-director for Kearney, Nebraska, T.R.A.C.

They munched on chocolate in the Fireside Room at camp. A "junk food buffet" awaited tired counselors and staff during brief breaks throughout the three-day weekend.

"It makes me wonder how many people fully realize the ramifications of abuse, neglect and drug and alcohol addiction," Lisa said as they talked about the histories of some of the teens.

Angela thought about the details on campers' applications. Half were doped on enough medications to fill a pharmacy.

"It's like we're on two different planets."

Angela nodded. Even after teaching four years at a middle school with a rough reputation, she still didn't grasp the depravity some of her students faced.

"Dysfunction rules the planet where these kids live." Lisa sighed. "I can't understand their planet any more than they understand how to function on my orderly planet."

Just Three Days

More than once, Lisa's analogy has come to Angela's mind.

Volunteering with foster teens at T.R.A.C. has opened her eyes — and her heart — to see the darkness God wants to illuminate.

Beautiful

"You are beautiful," Lauri, a Mary Kay consultant told the girls at Sherwood, Oregon, T.R.A.C. "Makeup simply enhances the beauty you already possess."

Small pink mirrors reflected intent listeners seated at a table in the activity center.

"I want you to look deeper," the camp volunteer continued. "We all have yuck inside us or yuck done to us. But God made us beautiful, and He washes the yuck away."

The girls stared into the mirrors, as if trying to see what Lauri described. Many lived in a pit of lies, believing they were ugly and worthless.

"Repeat after me," she said. "I am beautiful."

All but one voice repeated the words Lauri spoke. Tears ran down the cheeks of an overweight teen name Leila with a complexion the color of caramel. Head bowed, she wouldn't look in the mirror.

"What's wrong, honey?" Lauri asked.

"I can't say it," she sniffled. A lifetime of ridicule and insults made the words difficult for Leila to believe.

"But you're gorgeous."

"No, I'm not." She shook her head, and more tears

flowed. "I've done too many things. And things have been done to me."

"Leila, no matter what others have said or done to you," Lauri's voice softened, "to God, you are beautiful."

"Yeah," the others echoed. "You're beautiful."

"I want you to practice," Lauri encouraged. "Practice saying you're beautiful."

Finally, after much support, the girl looked into the mirror and said, "I believe God made me beautiful."

Mascara ran in rivers down her face, but Leila didn't mind. She shined behind the makeup Lauri lovingly reapplied.

Part Two: The Story of Joseph

Dear T.R.A.C.,

Thank you so much for everything! This has truly been an amazing experience for me. I have never felt love from a guy (dad) and Will, Jess, Scott and Grandpa all made me feel loved. When you guys all said that I was beautiful, I had a hard time because I thought you guys were told to say that. I have a really hard time trusting people, and you have helped me trust more. Thank you for talking about forgiveness. I have been hurt so many times, and you have given me some confidence in forgiving my dad. I love you guys! Thank you!

Shawna

Billboard

Along Interstate 80 in Omaha, Nebraska, a billboard catches your attention. Sponsored by a faith-based group, the sign features a young girl with dark eyes. The caption next to her is haunting.

My bucket list:

1. Find something to eat today.
2. Find a way to school.
3. Protect my sister from my mom's boyfriend.
4. Stay alive.
5. Turn 16.

The counselors at Omaha T.R.A.C. tell a similar story. One year, they asked their campers to write their dreams on a sticky note to tape inside their Bibles.

"I hope I graduate," Chelsea piped up. "If I do, I will be the first in my family."

"I don't have any dreams," a 13 year old said. She refused to write a thing.

Part Two: The Story of Joseph

Another year, the counselors asked the girls to write qualities they wanted in a future husband. The counselors expected responses similar to their own lists — tall, dark, handsome man who loves God and sweeps me off my feet.

Instead, the responses revealed a deeper longing.

1. Doesn't abuse me.
2. Has a job.
3. Doesn't drink.
4. Doesn't do drugs.
5. Won't leave me.

God is present in the darkness, and He pursues the hurting. T.R.A.C. points foster teens out of the pit to a path illuminated with His truth.

The Piano

"Don't worry. I ain't got no family," Jamal rapped on stage. "Wait, T.R.A.C. is my family."

The audience at the talent show cheered for Jamal. Despite several failed adoptions, the confident African-American teenager encouraged everyone he met.

Mary, the campground director, listened to Jamal's story woven into the rap he'd composed. Tears welled up in her eyes. Later she learned Jamal could play the piano by ear without having had formal training.

"Do you care if I buy Jamal a keyboard?" Mary approached Kelli, who ran the T.R.A.C. program for Glendale, Arizona.

Kelli raised her eyebrows.

"He's touched my heart."

Mary purchased two keyboards — one for the campground and one for Jamal. When Jamal got off the bus after T.R.A.C., two volunteers walked with him to the car where they presented him with the keyboard. Jamal couldn't believe it.

Today, after three years at T.R.A.C., Jamal has a mentor and is part of the Life Skills Program at Arizona's

Hope & A Future. He is learning that, like Joseph, God is with him even in the darkness. His goals: 1. to apply for one of two four-year college scholarships provided by Grand Canyon University to graduates of the Life Skills Program, and 2. to make lots of money to give to charities like T.R.A.C. so they can continue doing what they're doing.

Last Minute Counselor

"I think I'm supposed to help at camp," Peggy blurted into the phone a few weeks before Kearney, Nebraska, T.R.A.C. Volunteering with Royal Family KIDS motivated her and her husband to be foster parents. After raising their own kids, the couple welcomed teen boys into their home.

Angela, co-director, sat up in bed, wiping the sleep from her eyes. Blurry red lines on the clock became numbers when she grabbed her glasses.

"Sorry it's so early," Peggy rushed. "But I felt God prompting me, and I wanted to act before I changed my mind. I'll help wherever you need me."

"How about being a counselor?" Angela found her voice. "Two more camper applications just came in the mail."

Peggy called a few days later. "I just heard Ginny's coming. My niece still keeps in touch with her, even though Ginny's back with her mom."

Angela found Virginia on the girls' roster. Peggy had been the quiet girl's "big camper" (counselor) at Royal Family KIDS.

Part Two: The Story of Joseph

"I didn't know Ginny was coming when I volunteered. Now I know why God wants me at T.R.A.C.; Ginny never thought we'd see each other again."

Her next words made Angela want to hurl.

"Ginny's grandfather was in the paper. He's in jail because he paid her $5 every time he wanted sex."

Anger competed with Angela's disbelief. Sometimes the details were too much. Yet these same details haunted T.R.A.C. campers.

Ginny connected easily with Peggy. The night of the Princess Party, Ginny looked radiant in her formal gown. The picture of her and Peggy at the gazebo is one of many Ginny can add to her Royal Family KIDS albums, positive memories of hope, reminding Ginny her past doesn't have to define her. Like with Joseph, God can make good come from what was intended to harm.

Just Three Days

Dear T.R.A.C.,

Thank you for making me feel like I'm special and no one can take my place. I also thank you for making me feel beautiful. I haven't felt that way in a long time. Thank you for all the fun and taking time to spend with me.

Ginny

A Wish

Jamie watched *Facing the Giants* on Friday night along with the other campers at Sherwood, Oregon. This was the third year the determined girl with scraggly brown hair and glasses attended camp.

During one scene, the camera panned to a father standing in the end zone with his hands raised. He nodded his head as if to say, "You can do this, son." At that moment, the smallest member of the team kicked the winning field goal.

"I wish I had a dad like that," a voice rose above the others.

"Me, too," another camper agreed.

Jamie listened to the cry of her own heart, but said nothing. Earlier, she'd confessed never being able to forgive her father for the things he'd done.

On Sunday, Kaci led Cross Talk. She talked about her own experience growing up in a violent house. "How many of you walk by a wall in your home and cringe because you've been thrown against that wall?"

Many of the girls in the audience nodded.

"I'm here to tell you," Kaci spoke with authority, "life

doesn't have to be that way. Someday you get to make the rules — just like I did."

Hope shined on faces.

"In my house, hitting and violence are not allowed," Kaci said. "In my house, we love, and we encourage, and we offer forgiveness. No one is perfect, and sometimes we mess up. It's not easy to forgive, so we have to ask Jesus for help."

Jamie listened intently.

Kaci looked across her audience with compassion in her eyes. "Healing begins the very second you forgive. When your burden is lifted, then you are free to live the great life God has planned for you."

Later Jamie talked with her counselor. "Kaci's right. I want to have the best life. Can you help me pray?"

A radiant Jamie returned to camp the following year. Attendees at the annual T.R.A.C. banquet heard her testimony, "Jesus changed my life." That spring, she asked camp grandparents David and Peggy to attend her baptism. Like Joseph, Jamie knew the pit of rejection, but she chose forgiveness, and it made all the difference in her life.

The Manicure

"Two dollars for you. I do your nails." Terresa, Cross Talk teacher at Scio, Oregon, T.R.A.C., had fun doing the girls' nails.

"Why are you talking like that?" a camper asked.

"I'm mimicking my favorite manicurist who speaks in broken English." Terresa went back to her acting. "I tell you. You need massage. You skin so dry. It's no good."

Sadie giggled. The sweet blond, blue-eyed girl had taken a liking to Terresa. Without her sister at camp, she couldn't disappear into the shadows like in the past.

"What?" Terresa feigned shock. "You don't think a Mexican lady can impersonate an Asian?"

Sadie and the other girls couldn't stop laughing. "You're so crazy."

"Of course, I'm crazy." Terresa grinned. "God made me that way. I love it. I embrace it. I am crazy."

The revelation hit Sadie. "You can be crazy and talk about God and the things He does for us and have fun?"

"Of course." Terresa painted another girl's nails, then frowned at the color. "Do over. That color is all wrong for you." She grabbed the nail polish remover. "I'm so sorry, hon. Obviously, I'm not a professional."

Again Sadie couldn't hold her shock. "You didn't freak out?"

"Because I made a mistake?" Terresa sent the girls into more laughter with a half-snort. "It's okay to be wrong."

Sadie leaned back and studied her painted nails. Terresa could almost see a light bulb over Sadie's head. *Wow! It's okay to be wrong. And it's okay to love God and have fun, too.*

Simple truths, really. T.R.A.C. shined light into the pit of darkness.

Troublemaker?

"Is this Angela?" the voice on the phone asked.

"Yes," the co-director of Kearney, Nebraska, T.R.A.C. answered. "Who is this?"

"Annie. Billy's aunt."

Every time Angela thought of Billy, she remembered the talent show at Royal Family KIDS Camp. The tall, skinny kid with glasses missed nearly every note when he played a song on the piano, but he beamed at the audience's praise.

"I'm not sending Billy to T.R.A.C. this year." Frustration seeped through his aunt's words. "He was nothing but trouble at Boy Scout camp and horrible for a school trip to Washington, D.C."

Angela hoped Billy and his sister, Linda, weren't listening in the background.

"I just don't know what to do with him," she continued. "Everyone said they'd help me when his mom went to prison, but it's just me and my husband."

"I think Billy will do great at T.R.A.C." Angela redirected the conversation. Aunt Annie loved the martyr act. "We didn't have any problems last year, and our low camper-to-adult ratio helps kids like Billy."

Annie gave a humph. "Well, if you want him ..."

"Yes," Angela jumped in. "We can't wait to see Billy at camp."

Billy didn't cause any trouble at T.R.A.C. In fact, he warmed his way into most volunteers' hearts with his sweet nature and polite manners. Before he got on the bus, Billy thanked Angela for letting him come to camp.

"I'm so glad you came." Angela gave him a side hug. "You're a good kid. Don't forget that. No matter what *anyone* says."

Understanding sparked when their eyes locked.

Three days can illuminate the darkness.

Tree Weaving

Ida wove a colored strip of fabric into a loom stretched between two trees at Ventura, California, T.R.A.C. Like the other campers, she'd written a prayer onto her fabric using a colored Sharpie marker.

As Ida wove the color back and forth, the art teacher, Candi, explained how life came with its ins and outs, ups and downs.

The 13 year old with piercing green eyes refused to look at Candi.

"You don't have to share your prayer." The art teacher sensed Ida's pain. "But Jesus wants you to leave your hurts in His lap."

Tears welled in the camper's eyes as she finished weaving her fabric. "I feel so bad. I lost my virginity last year."

"God forgives you yesterday, today and tomorrow," Candi encouraged.

Ida found her counselor and cried for more than 45 minutes off to the side.

Candi could almost see Ida leave behind her shame as other campers wove their fabric into the tree weaving. When the last finished, Candi pointed to the completed product. "Look at the whole piece, girls. See how the dark specks highlight the light?"

Smiles lit several faces.

"The dark becomes a part of who we are. When we take a step back, the entire work becomes a work of beauty."

Ida and Candi exchanged a look; understanding sparked in Ida's eyes. God could make the dark places shine with His light, and her life, too, would reflect beauty.

70s Commercial

"I hope you consider coming back next year." Carol Joy, director of Hood River, Oregon, T.R.A.C., gave Tasha a side hug.

As they walked toward her foster parents, Tasha stopped mid-step and lifted her face to the heavens. She raised her hands and threw back her head in genuine ecstasy. "I can come back to camp when I'm 13. I can return when I'm 14. And I can come again when I'm 15."

Carol Joy blinked back her surprise. Three days earlier, Tasha had walked off the bus scowling. "Unless we're headed to the mall at this camp, I don't want to be here." When introduced to her counselor, Tasha said, "I hate the name April, and I hate you."

Now Tasha beamed. The moment was so surreal, Carol Joy felt like she was watching an old 70s commercial where the actors ran through the grass in slow motion, joy radiating from their faces.

Carol Joy worked hard at locating Tasha the next three years. Like many campers, she'd changed caseworkers and moved multiple times.

Over three summers, Tasha witnessed God's plan for

marriage. Her counselor, April, fell in love with a facilitator the first summer, got married the second and had a baby the next. The stability gave Tasha hope that life didn't have to be lived in the pit of despair. Three days can impact a life.

Garage Sale?

"Are you having a garage sale?" Will and Angela's neighbor Rachel called out from across the street as they loaded 64 prom dresses into the trailer normally used for BMX racing.

Will, co-director of Kearney, Nebraska, T.R.A.C., laughed. "No, we're pampering the foster girls coming to camp."

"Need any more dresses?" Rachel asked. Five minutes later, she returned with a pretty peach-colored formal. "I thought I had more, but I realized they're all at my mom's house."

Two days later, Brelynn slumped across the bunk in the girls' cabin.

"What's wrong?" her counselor, Vanessa, asked.

Brelynn didn't answer, so Vanessa sat on the bunk across from her. "I like the dresses." Brelynn's tough exterior cracked. "I just don't like me in them."

Vanessa heard the other girls squealing from the main room. "What if I bring in a couple other dresses?" she suggested. "Sometimes it takes longer to find the perfect dress."

"Whatever." Brelynn shrugged. Tears would stain her dark cheeks and leave her vulnerable — something she hated with two younger sisters, also at camp. Unlike her, they were white like their mother.

Three dresses later, Brelynn stared at herself in the mirror.

"You look beautiful," Vanessa gasped. "Let's go show the others."

Brelynn walked into the main room where Scott and Sara, a facilitator couple, waited on the couch.

Scott whistled. "Look at you."

"I look bad." Brelynn frowned.

"Whatever." Scott didn't buy her attitude. "You know you look good."

A smile tugged at the corners of Brelynn's mouth, and she twirled around. She wore the last dress donated — the peach-colored dress from Rachel.

The following year, a surgical procedure prevented Brelynn from attending girls' camp. Though she was disappointed, Brelynn gave up her spot to a neighbor in their trailer court. When she and her mom picked up her sisters after camp, a surprise awaited her: Brelynn got to choose a dress from the trailer.

When she emerged from the church bathroom in a flowing red gown, staff oohed and ahhed. This time, Brelynn immediately accepted the praise.

Her mom, Kim, handed the directors the following note.

Part Two: The Story of Joseph

I just wanted to let you and all the people involved with T.R.A.C. camp (know) how much joy you bring to mine and my daughters' lives. My girls look forward to your invite every year. Brelynn was very sad that she could not make it this year due to surgery, but she was happy that you were able to take Stephy in her place. Thank you. Your group truly brings tears to my eyes as I think about the things that you can provide my children, like an absolute fun weekend, positive male role models, the joy of in-love and married couples and above all the unconditional faith in God. Thank you for all you do.

Breylynn didn't have to wallow in a pit of lies. T.R.A.C. helped her see the truth.

Remembering to Pray

"I'm an atheist." Mason hid behind a hooded sweatshirt at Ventura, California, T.R.A.C.

Craig, his counselor and a new believer himself, listened. He didn't try to push Mason into participating in activities, including Cross Talk, or comment at the satanic images Mason drew during art.

After camp, Craig put a daily reminder on his computer to pray for Mason. He beamed when Mason stepped off the bus the following year.

"I'm so glad you're here." Craig clasped hands with Mason. "I've been praying for you all year."

A cheerful teenager smiled back.

Someone remembered him. He wasn't forgotten. The hooded sweatshirt came off, and Mason joined the others, eager for camp.

What If?

"Do you care if I change the direction of Cross Talk today?" Kathie asked T.R.A.C. directors, Dan and Sharla, at Sherwood, Oregon. "God woke me up at four this morning. And I feel like I'm supposed to share some things from my life." Dan and Sharla agreed.

A few hours later, Kathie stood in front of the campers. "What if you've lied? What would God say?"

"You're forgiven," a camper ventured.

"Exactly. Just like we've been talking about." Kathie nodded. "What if you've stolen things?"

"You're forgiven," more voices answered.

"What would God say if you've done inappropriate things with boys?"

"You're forgiven."

Kathie took a seat, letting her legs dangle off the stage. "What would God say if I wanted to kill myself?"

"Don't," several voices rushed at once.

Kathie searched the earnest faces and saw herself. "That's how I used to feel."

"God would say He created you," a girl pleaded. "He wants you to know He loves you and doesn't want you to kill yourself."

Later that afternoon, the campers stood on the challenge course. A sunbeam highlighted a clump of ferns. "This challenge is called the spider web," the facilitator explained. "You're going to help each other pass through the ropes."

Some of the girls looked doubtful.

"You can do it," he encouraged.

The campers worked together, cheering when the last girl emerged.

"Life is a lot like this web." The group huddled together to debrief the activity. "How many of you have gone through hard stuff?"

Hands shot up in the air.

A camper cleared her throat. "You know how Kathie said she wanted to kill herself?"

Her peers nodded.

"I wanted to commit suicide, too," she admitted.

"Me, too," another revealed.

Birds sang in the trees above as one camper after another opened her heart.

"Remember, you're not alone," the facilitator echoed the earlier Cross Talk lesson. "We all have trials like Joseph. But with Jesus' help, we can pass through to a new life."

Cousins

Tracy took a seat next to Mathias on the porch outside the cabins at Kearney, Nebraska, T.R.A.C. The other campers alternated between horseplay and changing into swim trunks.

"How's it going, man?" the long-time volunteer with Royal Family KIDS asked. Being a T.R.A.C. counselor brought new challenges for Tracy, including the impenetrable wall he sensed in the quiet, serious kid next to him.

"I've seen you before," Mathias said. "When I was with my foster mom. You were talking to her."

Tracy remembered Mathias. He'd been inspecting a home when he'd seen Peggy and Mathias. "Yeah, I was working that day."

"How do you know Peggy?" Mathias asked.

"She's my cousin."

The introspective 15 year old suddenly lit up. "So, that means we could be family, too." His dark eyes shined behind his glasses. "Cousins — real cousins — if I get adopted."

Adoption was a pretty big "if" to someone so late in his teens, but Tracy saw the longing on Mathias' face.

"Yeah." Tracy nodded. "I guess we'd be related, cuz."

A deep connection sparked between the two. Tracy knew his role as counselor was no accident. Four days before camp, three male counselors backed out. Without the great need, Tracy would have been placed in a different position. Seeing God's hand at work was both humbling and amazing.

Later Mathias' foster mom told the directors Mathias kept seeing this light after camp. "Something's different about him," she said. "It's like in the Bible when Paul saw the light on the road to Damascus. Mathias didn't want to be gone for three days, but camp made a difference in his life."

The closer the adoption/guardianship got, however, the more Mathias distanced himself from Peggy and her husband, Mark. Even after running from their home, though, Mathias knew he could count on them. "Can I come live with you again? I miss you and the things you stand for." He had some questions about the Bible and wanted to learn more.

"It's like Mathias views attachment to us as betrayal to blood relatives," Peggy observed. "But we told him we loved him even after he ran, and I think he needed to hear that in person."

For Mathias and other foster teens, issues of abandonment shake their very core. T.R.A.C. exposes them to the truth, shedding light into the darkness.

The Paintball Guy

Paul called his friend Jason on the phone after Sherwood, Oregon, T.R.A.C. He'd volunteered at camp for three years at the paintball venue. The wooded area was a favorite with teens who shot at tin cans and other targets. "I want what you have."

"What do you mean?" Jason, a camp counselor, asked.

"You and the staff at T.R.A.C. act different," Paul said. "I'm missing something. I'm happy with work and making money, but I don't have what you guys have. That's what I want."

Jason invited Paul to church.

Paul showed up on Sunday and accepted Jesus as His Savior.

Foster teens aren't the only ones impacted by camp. Adults also confront the ache in their hearts. Many leave camp forever changed, touched by the same God Joseph served.

Trying to Hide

"No." C.J. shook her head. "I'm not going to do this."

Cindy, director of The Woodlands, Texas, T.R.A.C., breathed a silent prayer. *What could she say to encourage this girl who deliberately tried to hide in oversized shirts and long athletic shorts?*

"I won't feel comfortable in a dress. I'll hate it."

"Okay," Cindy agreed. "I just don't want you to feel left out when everyone else is dressed up."

C.J. considered Cindy's concern.

"What if we buy you a new outfit? Like capris and a nice blouse?"

"What are capris?" C.J. hesitantly agreed.

A delighted Cindy headed to the store.

The evening of the dance, C.J. emerged from her room, clearly uncomfortable at the stares. Her limp foot dragged behind her. "What do you think?" she asked a friend.

"You look great."

"Really?" C.J. grunted.

She let the staff touch her lips with gloss and even relented to eye shadow. C.J. danced only one dance, but she was elated with her new pair of Vans tennis shoes. They'd been presented on a pillow, along with the other girls' formal shoes. The next morning, she promptly put on her new clothes.

Only God could have paired C.J. with her counselor the following year. C.J., who now wore a leg brace, easily identified with Michelle whose daughter wore the same style of brace.

"I was sexually molested by my grandfather," C.J. confided in Michelle when they were talking about forgiveness.

Michelle put a hand on C.J.'s shoulder.

"I don't have problems forgiving him." C.J. sighed. "I know my grandpa has problems. It's my father I can't forgive."

Michelle breathed a prayer for C.J.

"My dad never defended me." C.J. swallowed a lump in her throat. "When I told him what happened, he called me an ugly, stupid, lazy liar. He told me to get out of the house."

Michelle hugged C.J. for a long time.

That night at the dance, C.J. didn't hide. She wore a dress, and her eyes beamed from the compliments.

"You are an amazing young lady," Michelle told C.J.

C.J. smiled, facing the rejection from her earthly father in the light of God's love. "I know that now."

Hundred Dollar Bill

"We should use that object lesson we saw at directors' training," Angela mentioned to Will after remembering the illustration they'd seen with the hundred dollar bill.

A week later, Will received a card from a member of the spinning class he taught at the gym.

"You won't believe this." Will handed the envelope to Angela. A hundred dollar bill fell into her lap. "There's a Benjamin in there."

A month later, Will faced the audience at the awards ceremony for Kearney, Nebraska, T.R.A.C. "Would anybody like this?" He waved the hundred dollar bill in the air.

"Me, me, me!" Hands shot up around the room.

"What if I crumple it?" Will wadded the bill in his hand. "Anyone still want it?"

Boys jumped out of their seats. "I do!" they echoed.

Will spit on the money. Then he dropped the bill on the floor and ground it with his foot.

"What about now?"

"I'll take it." The excitement level rose even higher. "Give it to me!"

Part Two: The Story of Joseph

"But why do you still want it?" Will asked. "It's been wadded up, spit on and ground in the dirt."

A voice rose above the others. "Because it's still $100."

"Exactly," Will agreed. "The money has value — no matter what's happened to it."

Several counselors and staff eyed one another, realization dawning.

Will searched each face, knowing the pit of lies many believed. "Just like you."

Silence descended in the room.

"It doesn't matter what's happened to you." Will choked up. "You still have value."

A Peek

The petite girl with black hair was the most withdrawn girl in the group at Sherwood, Oregon, T.R.A.C. Her hard exterior pushed others away, keeping her trapped in a pit of pain and isolation.

On the last day of camp, the group met for challenge course.

"This is the spider web," Don, the facilitator, explained to the girls. "The goal is to get everyone through the web of ropes. When you pass through the center to be caught on the other side, I want you to release something. Something you want to leave behind."

Melinda was the last to be lifted up. When she emerged on the other side, she broke into tears. "I don't want to leave camp," she confessed. She opened her arms to hug the others.

"God changes the heart," a counselor who witnessed the change in Melinda later observed. "We can't always see results in three days, but once in a while, we get a peek."

The Apartment

Fear prickled Carol Joy's skin as she drove up to the rundown apartment building in a rough section of Portland. A car full of tough-looking men eyed her and Missy, the camper she was returning home. Somewhere a baby cried.

"Is this it?" Carol Joy pulled into a parking stall.

Missy nodded. "We're on the first floor."

Carol Joy stifled the panic she felt rise. Break-ins would be more likely on ground level. It was Sunday afternoon. She couldn't imagine the place shrouded in the dark of night.

Missy's foster mom answered the door. She especially grateful for the half-sheet of poster with the Biblical meaning of Missy's name. "Thank you. I'm going to put this on her wall. It's the only thing I have to decorate her room."

Carol Joy gave Missy a hug and held it together until she pulled out of the parking lot. As camp director, she preferred ignorance when it came to the particulars in the lives of her campers. Carol Joy hated suffering. It was the same reason she'd gone into research medicine rather than nursing.

Tears ran down Carol Joy's cheeks.

Missy had endured things no girl should experience. Even the other campers who'd been sexually abused couldn't handle the details Missy shared at Hood River, Oregon, T.R.A.C.

"Why, God? Why?" she screamed in silence.

Sin, rebellion, man's free will.

The Sunday school answer spoke to Carol Joy's head, not her heart.

She wanted to shut out the suffering. Squeeze her eyes shut and forget.

I love Missy.

A hot coal touched Carol Joy's soul.

I died for the abused ... and the abuser.

For just a moment, she tasted the suffering of her Savior. Of Missy's Savior.

Carol Joy drove out of the city and back to the country. Gradually her spirit quieted.

A memory came to mind of Missy terrified and curled into a fetal position on a bench at the horse venue.

Missy had conquered her fear and mounted a horse. She'd gotten so excited, she rode the animal into the nearby challenge course. The others could only gape in amazement.

Carol Joy grinned. Missy had also overcome her frustration at archery and aimed at the flying pig, a target mounted on a pulley. Other pictures of the girl filled Carol Joy's mind.

Part Two: The Story of Joseph

Missy smiling.

Missy laughing.

Missy enjoying life.

I love Missy, Jesus reminded Carol Joy. *I brought her to camp. I am with her even in the darkness. I will never abandon her. With Me, even what was meant for harm can be made good.*

God Hears

Becca stood before the girls at The Woodlands, Texas, T.R.A.C. and signed the words to the worship songs for Yvonne, a camper who was deaf.

While music notes swirled around the room, Becca's hands moved rhythmically in a silent choreographed dance.

Yvonne's lips moved as the sign language took on meaning.

"Are you Yvonne's interpreter?" An older camper named Danielle approached the two after the lesson on Joseph and forgiveness at Cross Talk.

Becca nodded.

"Can you interpret something to Yvonne for me?"

Becca readily agreed, touched that a camper who didn't know Yvonne would take the time to communicate with her.

Danielle turned to face the camper, who responded with a shy smile. "I want you to know that even though you can't speak or hear, God can still hear your voice."

Becca's hands moved furiously as Danielle continued. "During the worship, God was standing right next to you, and He loves you so much."

Part Two: The Story of Joseph

Becca could hardly finish signing the words without breaking down with emotion.

Cindy, the director, later shared the story with Danielle's adoptive mom who responded with the following e-mail:

> Cindy,
>
> Thank you for sharing this with me ... I cried and cried ... Thank you for providing a place where her faith could be nurtured in such a way. You have done miracles with my children who have been to your camp.
>
> Sally

The same God who sees every simple act of kindness hears every heart.

Memory Banks

During the bus ride home after Kearney, Nebraska, T.R.A.C., the campers burst into spontaneous singing. Instead of singing popular songs from the radio, the campers sang songs from Royal Family KIDS Camp and T.R.A.C. The full impact hit the staff later. These teens — whose backgrounds were darkened by abuse and neglect — held songs of hope and light embedded in their memory banks.

Wrong Camp

"My caseworker sent me to the wrong camp," Amiya exclaimed as soon as she walked off the bus.

Kelli, director of Glendale, Arizona, T.R.A.C., noted the sadness in Amiya's eyes. "I'm sorry you feel that way, but I hope you have fun, anyway."

Amiya went through the motions at camp. She never smiled, even during the pampering session at the Princess Program. Dressed in her gown, Amiya followed the other girls and staff out of the cabins.

Suddenly Amiya stopped. From the top of the ridge, she saw a red carpet. On either side, 20 guys dressed in black with pink ties waited to escort the girls into the open dining area.

"Why are you doing this for me?" Amiya shrank back. "I don't deserve any of this."

Amiya's counselor, Aimee, wrapped an arm around her. "You are beautiful." Stars twinkled in the early evening sky. "The maker of the world thinks you're beautiful. You do deserve this."

Amiya broke down in sobs. When she quieted, the staff fixed her makeup once again, and she walked down the red carpet. A small smile crept across her face.

Just Three Days

During the following two days of camp, Amiya blossomed. A smile stretched from ear to ear. She and Jana, another camper who'd been withdrawn for most of camp, had questions about God, so Aimee shared what Jesus had done in her own life and how much Jesus loved them. Hope shined in both girls.

Two weeks later, Amiya's survey arrived in the mail. "Prior to camp, I didn't want to live," she wrote. "Now I do."

Three months later, a staff member saw Amiya. The blankness was gone. She'd found hope outside of the pit. Life beamed from Amiya's eyes.

Aimee was so moved by her experience at T.R.A.C., she enrolled in school and graduated with a degree in family studies. Abuse had shattered her own marriage, and she wanted to help girls like Amiya know their identity in Christ. Aimee continues to volunteer at camp as the dean of women.

Three days impacts campers and volunteers.

Part Two: The Story of Joseph

Dear T.R.A.C.,

Thank you for teaching me how important it is to forgive people. I thank you for teaching me how beautiful I actually truly am, even though I may not see it. Thanks again for teaching me to turn to God and how important God really is to a young girl who is getting ready to go into high school. Going to high school and not having God in my heart, I wouldn't be who I am today, half the person... T.R.A.C. is a huge part of my life and has changed my heart. It has touched my heart and made me a wonderful young lady. Thank you.

Shannon

Auntie Lena?

"I know you can't share last names." Lena, a counselor, approached Angela Thursday night before campers arrived. "But I have to know. Is Channie my niece? Her name is so unusual, I've been thinking of her non-stop since I heard the name."

Angela, co-director/camper placement coordinator for Kearney, Nebraska, T.R.A.C., verified the truth the counselor already knew.

Tears filled Lena's eyes. "That's my brother's daughter."

The two exchanged a hug. After Lena's mother died and her father relinquished his parental rights, Lena and five siblings had been raised by different relatives than her brother and another sister. Lena regretted not having the opportunity to get to know her brother.

When alcoholism ended her brother's marriage, Lena's family lost contact with Channie and her older sister. Lena saw the girls at a school program when Channie was 9, but her attempt to reestablish a relationship met with resistance from Channie's mother. Two months before T.R.A.C., Lena learned Channie was in foster care. Finding out her niece had been raped broke her heart.

Part Two: The Story of Joseph

The first morning of T.R.A.C., campers and staff stood in a huge circle for an icebreaker. As campers and staff ran back and forth across the circle, at one point, Lena and Channie found themselves next to each other.

Lena gulped. "Hi, Channie."

The camper with the crooked smile cocked her head in confusion.

"It's me. Auntie Lena."

Channie stammered in disbelief, much like Joseph must've felt when facing his brothers again after years apart. The two embraced in sweet reunion.

"It's about lunchtime," Will, the co-director, announced from the middle of the circle. "Do I have any volunteers to pray for lunch?"

Silence descended on the large group. Channie looked at her aunt.

"Go ahead." Lena nodded.

Channie stepped forward. "I'll pray."

Later, when Channie tried on dresses for the Princess Party, she wanted Auntie Lena to see her in the sleeveless midnight-blue formal she'd selected. At lunch the next day, Channie ran up to give her aunt the biggest hug and kiss on the cheek. "I love you." The gestures touched Lena deeply, especially since she hadn't had the chance to let her niece know her absence from Channie's life wasn't by choice.

Lena and her husband, Jeff, completed foster parent licensing not long before T.R.A.C., and now they wondered if God's plan involved Channie all along. After calling six different numbers and talking with numerous people, Lena got in touch with Channie's caseworker. "I haven't heard back yet, but I'm not going to be the aunt in the background waiting for the next chance to see her," she told Angela. "I want to be a part of my niece's life."

Just as God worked full circle in Joseph's life, He is doing the same for Channie; Auntie Lena couldn't be more grateful for the connection made at T.R.A.C.

When the Nightmare Vanished

Screams woke Tim at four in the morning at Sherwood, Oregon, T.R.A.C. They were coming from one of the girls' tents.

"Jesus, fill this camper with the peace of Your holy presence." He prayed for 15 minutes until the intermittent screams quieted.

The next morning, a slender camper nicknamed Jules hurried to where Tim rang the breakfast bell. Rays of sunlight danced on the outdoor deck.

"Tim, you'll never believe what happened last night." The teen with blond hair beamed. "I saw my mom in my dreams."

Tim remembered the screams he'd heard.

"And I could finally tell her no," she rushed. "I had enough power inside of me to tell her God loves me."

As a young child, Jules was forced into posing for pornographic pictures and selling her body for sex to support her mother's drug habit. When her mother was finally imprisoned, Jules had all but disappeared into a shell of herself.

A lump lodged in Tim's throat. Jules' eyes were brighter than he'd ever seen. The broken girl he first met at Royal Family KIDS Camp wouldn't look anyone in the eye. But slowly, after seven years of camp, Jules gained confidence.

"When I woke up, I realized I had the same power inside me." Jules' voice rose in excitement. "It was all because of Jesus, so I asked Him into my heart. I want Him to be Lord of my life."

"That's wonderful." Tim gave Jules a side hug.

"That's not all, though," Jules continued, tears streaming from her eyes. "I told my mom I forgave her." She sniffled. "That's so important I tell her that."

After Cross Talk, Jules shared her story with the other girls in her tent. Peace flooded her face as she looked at the faces of her friends. "I think asking Jesus into our hearts is the best decision we can make in life," Jules finished. "Whenever you're ready, I'd like to challenge you to do the same."

Tim recalls the incredible presence of God at camp that year. In all, 10 other girls asked Jesus into their hearts. And for Jules, the nightmare finally vanished. She left the pit and never returned.

Part Three
A Well-Beaten Path:
Daniel and the Lions' Den

Teens in foster care can easily develop a "victim" mentality. Campers at T.R.A.C., however, are challenged, like Daniel, to see beyond their circumstances. Taken captive when Babylon besieged Jerusalem, Daniel acclimated to his new environment and stood firm in his faith in God. As a result, he was thrown into the lions' den, but God saved Daniel by sending an angel to shut the mouths of the lions.

Volunteers pour love into campers, emulating God's love. For many, distrustful of adults, seeing genuine love in action changes their perception of God. They learn Psalm 25:4-5, which reads, "Show me your ways, O Lord, teach me your paths; guide me in your truth and teach me, for you are God my Savior, and my hope is in you all day long." Campers begin to learn God is trustworthy.

A Handful of Rocks

"No one told me this was a Jesus camp," Rayford demanded after Cross Talk at Sherwood, Oregon, T.R.A.C. "I want to go home. I'm an atheist. Hitler's my hero."

"But we haven't even gone fishing," his co-counselor offered. He wasn't much bigger than the Hispanic kid.

"I don't want to be here." Rayford scowled. He picked up a handful of dirt and gravel and threw it, hitting his co-counselor in the face.

The behavior specialist intervened, and Dan, the director, called Rayford's mother. No one answered.

"Try again," Rayford hissed.

Dan punched in the number a second time.

Nothing.

"How about hanging out while I try to reach your mom?" Dan suggested.

Rayford reluctantly agreed. By the afternoon, however, his anger flared.

"I've called her several times," Dan told him. "Your mom's not answering."

"So, call her boyfriend," Rayford spit out. "He'll come get me."

"We can't," Dan explained. "He's not listed as the emergency contact."

Rayford grabbed a handful of rocks. "You can't keep me here. I'll throw these through a window." He aimed for the lodge, then glared at his small group. "Or one of you. I'll throw them at you."

His co-counselor grabbed Rayford in a bear hug. "Even if you do, I'll still love you."

"What?" He jerked back, growling. "What do you mean?"

"I'll still love you," the co-counselor repeated. "No matter what you do."

The response took Rayford off guard. One by one, the rocks dropped out of his hand.

Rayford's attitude shifted. At mealtimes on the deck which overlooked camp, he relived his fun with the others in his group. He even participated in the talent show, despite his earlier refusal. At Cross Talk, Rayford opened his Bible and followed along as Daniel's story unfolded.

"Daniel was kind of stupid," Rayford muttered under his breath. "But brave, too."

The boy who wanted to throw rocks left camp changed, challenged to trust the God he'd once rejected.

Part Three: Daniel and the Lions' Den

Dear T.R.A.C.,

Thank you for everything. I've really been struggling with my rape that happened recently. I felt like I wasn't pretty at all. Coming here really showed how truly beautiful I am ... I forgive God for what I had to go thru. I am truly a survivor — not a victim!

Cassie

Golden Memories

Dirk spent most of the first day of camp at the hospital after twisting his ankle. The staff at Glendale, Arizona, T.R.A.C. worried the tall athletic kid might miss out on basketball tryouts for school because of the injury, but Dirk stopped hobbling on his crutches by the third day.

After the last Cross Talk, Dirk's group returned to their cabin. Like Daniel, many had been thrown into the lions' den, and they shared obstacles they'd faced.

"I need to forgive my mom for choosing drugs over me," Dirk opened up. "She abandoned me when I was 5."

Discarded clothes and wet swim trunks lay around the cabin, but no one moved to pack up. Dirk continued to pour out his heart as everyone sat together at the table. "My aunt took me in, but she treated me like a burden, not part of the family."

Several boys nodded in understanding.

"I got stuck in foster care when my mom severed her rights to me, but not my brother or sister." Dirk sighed. "I don't know if I'll ever see her again."

"Wow. Sometimes I think I got it rough." Evan, another camper, clicked his tongue. "But hearing you makes me appreciate my grandma. I need to tell her. I never realized what she did when she took me, my sister and younger brother in."

The two counselors eyed one another. Guys didn't have conversations like this — especially 15-year-old teenagers.

"God doesn't want me to carry this weight anymore," Dirk finished. "He wants me to forgive those who hurt me so I can move forward on my life's path."

A few hours later, the boys wished one another goodbye. "I'll never forget how important it is to forgive," Dirk told the group. "My memories at camp are golden."

Followers

Tim first met Dan when the two roomed together as staff members with their Royal Family KIDS campers. Dan's love for hurting kids was obvious, so Dan and his wife, Sharla, would be a natural fit with teens. Tim and Serena invited the couple to their home.

"Would you consider directing Sherwood T.R.A.C.?" Tim asked them over dessert. "God is expanding the vision of T.R.A.C., but we can't train directors and run camp at the same time. New directors would benefit by seeing a camp in action."

Dan and Sharla exchanged a look of surprise. "We're followers. Not leadership people."

Tim nodded slowly. He saw their passion, even if they could not. The two would make incredible leaders. "Could you pray about it? God keeps bringing you to mind."

Like Daniel, Dan and Sharla prayed. Because they obeyed, hundreds of teens across the nation now hear God loves them.

"If God's people don't say yes," Tim said, "things don't happen."

God works through followers who let Him lead.

Strange Pairings

Like many T.R.A.C. directors, Cindy can attest to the fact that grouping campers and pairing campers with counselors is a formidable task. Prayer — Daniel's mainstay — takes the pressure off. She and others spend hours seeking God.

At first glance, two matches at Woodlands, Texas, T.R.A.C. seemed especially strange.

Nate, an engineer volunteering as a counselor, was partnered with Alvin, a skater whose family had been evacuated because of Hurricane Katrina. How could Cindy know the skater wanted to be an engineer?

Alvin also bonded with a camper in his cabin who was a cowboy. The boys emerged as natural leaders on the challenge course.

"Dude," Alvin told the cowboy he misjudged as a redneck, "when I first saw you, I thought we didn't have anything in common. Now I have nothing but respect for you."

Sometimes, the pairings come with disappointment.

John, a counselor with a love for basketball, secretly

wished to be partnered with Manny, a tall black kid. Instead, John was paired with Demetrius, a kid with swollen ankles.

At lunch, John saw the meds Demetrius took and realized the two had the same gastro-intestinal issues.

"I understand exactly what this kid is going through. That was me as a kid." John grinned. "Turns out Demetrius loves basketball, too."

Only God can make matches like these.

Fish and Loaf Multiplication

"There's no way we can pull the Princess Party off." Angela frowned, crossing her arms.

Seven months after attending T.R.A.C. directors' training, she wondered how camp would get off the ground. Adding a formal evening for the girls would be nothing short of a miracle.

"Faith," her husband, Will, responded in his typical even-keeled manner. "We have to have faith."

"Easy for you to say," she shot back. "You start a new job, remember? You'll be gone for most of the planning." Weeks earlier, the National Guard had assigned Will to Offutt Air Force Base, three hours away from their home in central Nebraska.

Kearney's first camp was five months away.

Did we hear wrong? Angela asked God.

No, a voice sounded in her spirit. *T.R.A.C. is bigger than you. I called you to plant a camp. I can bring new directors in the future.*

Faith was a tall order. And Angela didn't feel much like Daniel, who never wavered in his faith.

"Remember the nudge we both felt at training?" Will asked.

Angela groaned. Life was wrecking havoc to their dreams.

"How?" Angela asked, her chest rising. "How do we make the Princess Party happen? We don't even have campers yet. Not to mention a hundred other details. And now we have a house to sell and boxes to pack. Camp itself might flop."

Will shrugged.

Great plan, Angela almost screamed. Sometimes her husband was impossible.

"I don't know the details," he said. "But God can do it."

"Fine," Angela huffed. "God's in charge of the Princess Party. I'm too busy surviving."

Fast forward to August.

White lights and tulle turned the camp dining room into a ballroom. Twenty-five teen girls traded their T.R.A.C. t-shirts for formal gowns, glittering tiaras and dainty double-stranded cross necklaces.

The transformation was surreal. The day before, Bob, the Cross Talk leader, had invited the same girls to leave their pain at the wooden cross overlooking the lake. Angry words scrawled in red marker — pain, abuse, rape — bled into the grain as girls returned to their seats, crying.

Now they danced with abandon to the Cha Cha Slide, the Flying Dutchman and the Macarena, like young girls, innocence restored. Johnny Diaz's song, "More Beautiful You," blared from the speakers as Will told each girl she was beautiful and handed her a CD of the song.

Part Three: Daniel and the Lions' Den

The next day, girls came to breakfast wearing their camp t-shirts and tiaras.

Will squeezed Angela's hand. "God is amazing."

She was too choked up to speak.

Later, when they packed up the dresses, Angela felt like Cinderella after the ball. *Had the magical evening really happened?*

As she took inventory, she stopped, sure she'd counted wrong. *How could there be more than 100 dresses? She and Will brought 65 dresses to camp in their trailer and gave away 25 to the girls. There should be 40 left — not 100.* Angela recounted. Sure enough. One hundred dresses lined the racks.

Angela's jaw dropped. The same God who saved Daniel still performed miracles. She'd just witnessed a modern day fish and loaf multiplication.

Pest Protection

Yellow jackets plagued camp one summer in Biblical proportions at Hood River, Oregon, T.R.A.C. Insecticide foggers and sprays made little difference.

At Cross Talk, Bob stood in front of his audience while yellow jackets swarmed around his face and crawled along his arms. Counselors and campers swatted at the pests, while the outdoorsy mountain climber didn't even flinch. Instead he used the opportunity. "God protected Daniel in the lions' den," he explained. "And He will protect us."

Bob was right. Not one camper got stung the entire three days.

Hate?

"I hate you, Denise!" Billie screamed without provocation at her counselor at Omaha, Nebraska, T.R.A.C. Gravel crunched under their tennis shoes as they strolled along the path which wound through camp.

Danielle, another counselor, tried to encourage Denise with her smile. The random outbursts were becoming common. Hatred met any kindness. Every 10 minutes, Billie yelled, "I hate you, Denise! And I hate your family, too!"

Years in foster care hardened the teenager. The family she'd been with for five years had been awarded guardianship, but Billie took pride in not wanting to be adopted.

The group arrived at the basketball court on the edge of the challenge course. "Hey, campers," the facilitators welcomed them. "Our challenge today involves building a free-standing tower with a marshmallow and raw spaghetti noodles." Jeff held up a stopwatch. "The catch: the clock is ticking."

"That's stupid," Billie muttered. She hoarded the materials while Denise attempted to build a tower with Chelsea, her other camper. Billie ate the marshmallow.

Things worsened the rest of the afternoon. Billie's negativity impacted the whole group. After the campers fell asleep, Denise and Danielle sat down on the cabin floor and cried.

Frustration welled up inside Denise. She wasn't new to volunteering with Royal Family KIDS or T.R.A.C., yet Billie wore her down.

"I don't know if I'll make it through two more days," she confided to Danielle. The two prayed, vowing to stand on God's grace which was new every day.

On Saturday, the girls set goals for their cabin as they headed to breakfast.

Without help, the girls decided on three things: 1. Have a positive mental attitude. 2. Finish everything they started. 3. Be respectful.

"What if we use hand signals for accountability?" Denise suggested.

The girls agreed, but by late morning, little had changed. The afternoon wasn't better. Billie had a meltdown when she whacked herself in the head with a flashlight she insisted on clipping to her nametag.

"It's been another rough day," Denise told the girls. "We're acting younger than the youngest girls, but if you can hold it together for the beauty night this evening, we'll do a special walk around camp with our flashlights." She and Danielle didn't tell the girls they would stop by the counselors' break area and get a candy bar.

Amazingly enough, Billie took the lead.

Candy bar eaten, Billie was back to her dramatics.

Part Three: Daniel and the Lions' Den

"My throat is constricting," she screamed in the cabin. "I'm allergic to Colgate."

Denise sighed. "You used the same toothpaste last night."

"I need a doctor right now." Billie dropped to the floor in hysterics and rocked herself. Her behavior scared the other girls.

Denise sat down and wrapped her arms around Billie. "Is your heart hurting because you have to go home tomorrow?"

"No!" Billie yelled.

The nurse and behavior specialist intervened.

The last day was a repeat. At the awards ceremony, Denise complimented Billie in front of the rest of the campers. "Billie is such a leader. I look forward to how God will use her."

Denise sat down, and Billie growled. "I hate you because you're making me cry."

"That's your choice," Denise answered patiently. "I still love you, no matter how much you hate me. And more importantly, God loves you."

When the bus pulled into the parking lot at Brookside Church, every camper had a ride except Billie. Tim, the director, left repeated messages for her foster parents, but no one came.

A docile Billie waited with Tim and Denise. "Tim, if I come back to camp next year, I want Denise to be my counselor again."

Denise broke down and wept.

Two hours later, Billie's foster parents finally showed up.

After T.R.A.C., Denise quit her job as an engineer to become a foster parent. Five years earlier, she would have laughed at the idea. Denise made changes to her home and lived on her savings, trusting God to provide. Soon after completing foster parent training, Denise received an offer for an engineering job with better hours. Within weeks, Denise got the news. Her first two foster teens would be arriving.

The brothers — Dante and Wayne — had attended Omaha's Royal Family KIDS Camp. Denise distinctly remembered Dante's concern for his younger brother. During activity time, she saw the pressure Dante put on himself when he got frustrated because his green paint strayed out of the lines. *This boy needs someone in his life,* she recalled thinking.

The fleeting notion returned to Denise's mind, along with a question she'd been asked at the combined interview for Royal Family KIDS/T.R.A.C.

"Are you willing to go on this journey wherever God takes you?"

Denise didn't hesitate, little realizing how life would change. Like Daniel, Denise responded in obedience to God's leading.

Camp doesn't just impact kids like Dante and Billie.

It changes the hearts of God's servants.

Part Three: Daniel and the Lions' Den

Dear T.R.A.C.,

Thank you for making me realize how I can trust people again. You showed me how to be a better person, how to be a better man. You made me realize how to forgive and forget. Thank you for making my last year awesome. I will never forget you; you are forever in my heart. Thank you, and God bless you.

Anthony

Determined to Return

"No one can make this look good." The tall African-American girl ran a hand through her short hair and frowned at the mirror.

"What? You don't know what you're seeing." Toni's friends pointed to her reflection. "You're gorgeous."

Cindy, T.R.A.C. director at The Woodlands, Texas, smiled. Each of the girls had a special place in her heart.

With this vote of confidence, Toni held a microphone several hours later. Her eyes gleamed under the lights at the dance.

"You've changed my life." Toni looked at Cindy. "Cindy, because of you and this camp, I know I am special and beautiful." Toni turned to the table where her friends sat. "I want all the girls in my cabin to stand up."

One by one, the girls stood.

Cindy's eyes fell on Mia, a petite girl with caramel-colored skin and dark hair. She and Toni had been plotting how to extend camp beyond the age of 15.

"You taught us God loves us." Toni's voice brought Cindy's thoughts back to the dance. "We're not alone. We're all special and beautiful. Thank you."

Pastor Wells, whose church sponsored The

Part Three: Daniel and the Lions' Den

Woodlands T.R.A.C., was at the dance. He leaned over to Cindy and whispered, "Now I know why you are doing this."

Me, too. Cindy didn't trust herself to speak.

The next day, Mia and Toni got ready to load the bus. "We'll do anything to come back," they'd pleaded. "Mop bathrooms, cook, anything."

What could Cindy say? "That wouldn't be right," she stammered.

"Then how old do you have to be to volunteer at T.R.A.C.?" Mia asked.

"Twenty."

Mia, who Cindy learned from her foster mom was ranked second in her class and determined to be valedictorian, smiled. "Then I'll see you in 2014."

The two returned the following summer as junior cousins (counselors) and blessed everyone. Not only did Toni and Mia help in all areas of camp, they brainstormed ideas for a camp ministering to 16-19 year olds. Knowing the girls, Cindy wouldn't be surprised if their ideas became reality as they continue to lean on God to guide them as Daniel did.

Who Do You Trust?

Kori, a counselor at Glendale, Arizona, T.R.A.C., didn't expect to freeze at the question posed on the challenge course. "Who do you trust when things are tough?"

When a camper deflected to Kori, she couldn't answer. Moving from Ohio to Arizona had been harder than she'd expected. Like Daniel must have felt when he was taken captive, she missed her family and friends back home. Away from the familiar, she clung stronger to God.

A long, vulnerable moment passed in silence. Finally, Kori shared her recent struggles of vulnerability.

"I felt so alone." Kori wiped at the tears rolling down her face. "If it wasn't for God, I don't know where I'd be."

That night, Kori returned from a break to find the following note on her bunk.

Kori,

I'm so glad I got to know you this year. You're a wonderful person with a kind heart that no one has. That's what I like about you. I can relate to all the thoughts you had because I got taken away from my family because they couldn't take care of me and because I got beaten every time my dad would do drugs.

I don't have anyone to trust. I thought I could trust my big sister, but sometimes she turns her back on me. The only person I can trust is the Lord. So there's some of my story. I hope you understand my story because I totally understood yours.

Love Always,
Lark

The Raffle Ticket

Laughter filled the church bus from Kearney, Nebraska. The occupants weren't teenage campers, but nine adults who'd agreed to be T.R.A.C. facilitators. They reminisced about the weekend challenge course training with Dennis Roach from Spokane, Washington.

"Now, I can't wait till camp." Sara's eyes danced.

"I thought we were just holding a bunch of ropes," Deone said. "I didn't realize what facilitators really do." She teased the directors about recruiting an old couple like her and her husband, Leo.

Talk turned toward the boys' camp. "If we're going to have a formal evening for the girls, we need to do something equally amazing for the boys," someone said.

Soon the brainstorming turned to a hog roast. "We can bury a hog and have a roast," Scott suggested. "That would go great with a survivor challenge."

"I know a pig farmer," Leo mentioned.

"Me, too," Nancy piped up. "I'll talk to him."

The idea was met with excitement. Boys wanted adventure as much as girls wanted to be pursued like princesses.

A survivor challenge and hog roast would appeal to

the deep longing in a boy's heart to know if he had what it took to be a man.

Two days later, a manila envelope arrived in the mail addressed to Angela, co-director. Curious, she opened it and immediately burst out laughing. She'd forgotten about the single raffle ticket she'd purchased from a friend's daughter. The prize: half a hog.

Not only does God shut the mouths of lions, He has a sense of humor.

Campground for Free

Sandy, director of Tyler, Texas, T.R.A.C., peered out at the lake and imagined teens playing on the water. The small retreat center set in the woods would be ideal for camp.

"Beautiful, isn't it?" The groundskeeper followed her gaze. The two had volunteered together for Royal Family KIDS.

"It's perfect," she agreed. "The kids will love it."

"You know, I tried to get T.R.A.C. going here when I worked with that adoption agency," Woody admitted. "But things didn't get off the ground like I hoped."

"Oh, yeah?"

A grin crept across Woody's face. "Maybe they will now."

Not long after, Sandy learned the center would host T.R.A.C.

"And, the best part," Woody said excitedly, "it's free the first year."

"Free?" Sandy choked out.

"Yep. The board says you just have to provide your own food."

Part Three: Daniel and the Lions' Den

Sandy was speechless. The God Daniel served continued to be in the miracle business.

Headline News

Serena's heart broke as she read a letter from a foster mother. Details jumped off the page. *Severely malnourished. Thirty pounds underweight. Major learning and behavioral issues. In and out of 18 homes in 12 years.*

Sometimes the information was too much to bear. The boy had made headline news when the state found him and his siblings locked in cages.

"I'm committed to Bailey," the foster mother wrote. "I've heard about your camp, and I want him to go."

Bailey arrived at Sherwood, Oregon, T.R.A.C. speaking low and slow. Socially behind, his behavior was almost autistic. One of his coping mechanisms was to act like he didn't hear. Deep in her spirit, Serena wondered how T.R.A.C. could impact a life so shattered by pain.

The following year, the teenager who showed up to camp didn't resemble Bailey at all. This young man had grown five inches, and his confidence soared. Hope shined from eyes that had been so empty. But the sweetest change was laughter; Bailey laughed throughout camp.

"I can't believe it," Serena told his foster mom. "You've done an amazing job."

Part Three: Daniel and the Lions' Den

Bailey's new mom got choked up. "I couldn't have done it without T.R.A.C. He came out of his shell after camp last year. Three days saved Bailey's life."

Pictures

At a kickoff for Royal Family KIDS and T.R.A.C., a woman approached Mike, one of the photographers at Kitsap County, Washington, T.R.A.C.

"I adopted a foster child," the woman said. "And the only pictures I have from his past are from camp."

The photographer, who spent hours watching camp through a camera lens, was reminded again of the simple ways we serve God. A photo captures precious memories of hope. When those memories are connected to a loving God, faith like Daniel's can grow.

New Co-Directors?

Will welcomed Andy and Nancy at the front door. Plastic crinkled underfoot as they made their way to the kitchen. Fresh paint lingered in the air.

"Sorry about the mess." He pointed to a seat on the couch crowded into the kitchen. "The realtor suggested we give the walls a new coat."

Will's wife, Angela, pulled out paper plates from the bare cupboards. Like Daniel, they would soon move to an unfamiliar place. "Thanks for coming to lunch." The couple was fast becoming family after two weekends at camp.

"So, when does the house go on the market?" Nancy asked.

"Two more weeks."

After a few questions about Will's new job in Omaha, most of lunch was spent reminiscing about camp.

Before Angela served dessert, Will had a question for the pair.

"Would you consider giving up your roles as facilitators to become co-directors?"

Nancy, normally the excitable one, got quiet. She loved volunteering with youth group and once confided how she prayed her husband, an introvert and computer techie, would find his niche in ministry.

Andy shared a rare insight. "I see things differently after camp." Not a touchy-feely type, he got ribbed by the staff for his big personal bubble. Andy's "behind the scenes" help and life experience, however, proved invaluable to a successful first year for Kearney T.R.A.C.

"Like when I see my nephews now." Andy paused, reflecting on the instability in the boys' lives. "I see their pain more. My understanding and love have grown."

A year later, Andy and Nancy flew to Oregon for directors' training. The two are now helping in youth together, and T.R.A.C. has become a perfect fit for the former airman and his outgoing wife.

One School

Amanda admired herself in the beautiful formal at Glendale, Arizona, T.R.A.C.

Kori, her counselor, smiled as she watched the girl in the mirror.

"I can't remember the last time I've been in a dress," Amanda confided.

The next day, the two chatted as they followed the others back to the cabin. Amanda wore the bow from the night before in her hair.

"So, what's next for you?" Kori asked.

"I'm hoping my adoption goes through," Amanda admitted. "I've been in nine different schools, and I'm struggling with my grades."

Kori tried to hide her surprise. *Nine schools? How often had Amanda found herself in the den of the lions?* The girl was only 13.

Camp ended, and Kori saw Amanda at a Christmas party for campers.

"I've been adopted," Amanda rushed to tell Kori. "I finally get to go to one school."

Just Three Days

Kori gave her a big hug. "So how are your grades?"

Amanda lit up. "I'm making all Bs."

Part Three: Daniel and the Lions' Den

Trail Ride

Deadline: today.

Jennie, director of **T.R.A.C.***life* in Sherwood, Oregon, scanned the last minute e-mail, wondering if she could get the paperwork done in time. Winning the grant worth $500 meant the teens could go to Badger Creek Ranch, a Christian horse ranch in Wamic, Oregon.

Seven months later, five teens — Angelica, Jami, Kaitlyn, Gary and T.J. — along with Jennie and their mentors made the two-hour trip to Wamic. Jennie couldn't be more thrilled. The trail ride, like camp, would be an experience these teens would not forget. After unloading their bags, the group played glow-in-the-dark whiffle ball in the corral, then roasted marshmallows and had a devotional.

The next day, a deer wandered up to the cook's shack while the group ate breakfast. T.J. fed it an apple from his hand. The at-risk teen frequently backed out of his mentor visits, but he'd come to the trail ride grudgingly.

"Before we take off, you need some training," Kenda, the co-owner of the ranch, explained to the group. She taught them how to hold the reins and give the horse commands. "Take some time getting to know your animal."

Kaitlyn twisted the long mane of her horse into a braid.

"She's pretty grumpy to start off with," Kenda said. "But if you're patient, you'll have a friend for life." She could've been describing Kaitlyn, the small muscular tomboy with the tough exterior.

"I'm not going." T.J. stuck his hands into the pockets of his low-hanging jeans. "Why can't I hitch a ride home? I got things to do."

"Come on," Jennie encouraged him. "You made a commitment, and we need everyone here to make this work. We need you and your mentor both."

T.J. slumped against the fence and messed with the ball cap he wore backward on his head. Swearing didn't get a response. He finally inched toward his horse when it was time to leave.

The trail led through rolling brown hills dotted with evergreens. Cattle ranches dominated the area, so the horses passed over several cattle guards. The city kids adapted quickly, except for T.J. who remained tense.

"I hear water," one of the girls piped up.

"That's the stream we'll cross," Kenda said. "Give the reins slack. The horses need to move their heads freely to find their footing." The splash of water filled the air. A few droplets landed on smiling faces.

For lunch, the group stopped in a grove overlooking

the hills. Kenda helped the kids tie the horses to the trees and pulled out picnic supplies from the saddlebags.

Thrashing and a loud squeal cracked the air.

"It's okay," Kenda reassured the teens. "The horse just got spooked." She soothed the animal with her words and cut the rope to prevent injury.

"It's the same with us and God." Kenda used the experience. "If we don't trust Him, we'll steer in the wrong direction and harm ourselves."

The teens — including T.J. — weren't ready to turn back. "I'm glad you came," Jennie told him.

"I still don't want to be here," T.J. teased, a huge grin plastered across his face.

No one could stop talking about the trail ride when they stopped for pizza. Jennie watched Jami show off her pictures to Charlotte, the woman who thought she was too old to be a mentor. The boisterous girl adored Charlotte's calm influence.

Angelica and her mentor, Vickie, also had a special relationship. Angelica had been baptized earlier in the year, and her sweet spirit and kind heart won a friend contemplating suicide to Jesus.

Jennie's heart swelled with gratitude. The entire group gelled easily since their first quarterly meeting. Launching the first **T.R.A.C.***life* program hadn't been easy, but seeing the growth made all the challenges fade. By pouring love into teens, mentors showed their mentees that the God Daniel trusted is still trustworthy.

Just Three Days

Dear T.R.A.C. Staff,

No matter how many times I say thank you, it will never be enough. I can't believe all the cool people who run the camp, taking time out of their busy schedules to hang out with a bunch of teenage foster kids like me so we can go to camp. This camp will change my life forever. I have made good friends at camp, and I have learned to trust others. I pray for all the people who do T.R.A.C.s across the country because I want more to start for kids like me.

Thanks again,
Jeffrey

Finding Purpose

Sitting around the Fireside Room after the campers fell asleep was becoming a tradition for the staff at Kearney, Nebraska, T.R.A.C.

Dead tired after two consecutive weekends of camp, people got loopy, and laughter filled the air. Chocolate and caffeine from the "junk food potluck" contributed to the fun.

"I gotta hand it to you, guys." Sara shook her head in disbelief at the male staff. "I didn't think you could pull it off tonight."

"Even with your detailed instructions?" Will, co-director, teased. Sara had written two pages of notes on decorating the dining room for the Princess Party while the women helped the campers get ready.

"I know my husband," Sara deadpanned. "I was worried."

Scott laughed the loudest. "And you were impressed, weren't you?"

Sara took a bite of her candy bar. "Immensely. Did you see the looks on the girls' faces?"

A brief silence descended as each one was lost in the memory of an enchanted night.

Tears welled in Sara's eyes. "You know, some people search their whole lives trying to find their purpose." She gulped. "I found my ministry at T.R.A.C."

I Like Me at Camp

"We've grown close at camp," Tommy, a T.R.A.C. volunteer for The Woodlands, Texas, told the girls the night of the dance.

Heads nodded in agreement, glitter sparkling from their jewelry. Formal dresses in a rainbow of colors contrasted with camp t-shirts and shorts worn earlier in the day.

"I wish I could be there when a guy comes to your house for a date," he continued.

Titters of anticipation zapped around the room.

"If I was there, this is what I would say to the young man." Tommy looked from face to face. "You are taking out a very special person. She needs to be treated with honor and respect." He raised his arm above his head and challenged them to set a high standard for themselves, like Daniel.

"The bar has been set this high. Don't ever allow anyone to treat you less than how you've been treated tonight."

Lori, an overweight camper, danced with abandon. The same girl had wanted to disappear after struggling on the challenge course her first year of camp.

"You look like you're having fun." Her counselor smiled.

"The time of my life." Lori's eyes gleamed. "I like me at camp. And that's the me I'm going to be at school next year."

Part Three: Daniel and the Lions' Den

Relating

Scott, director of Kitsap County, Washington, T.R.A.C., sighed as soon as the bus became a battlefield. The junior high teacher and former Navy Seal wondered how he could relate to Tamika and her two friends. Besides their different skin color, they had about as much in common as Daniel and his Hebrew friends had with the Babylonian culture.

Tamika frowned when Scott walked to the back of the bus. Two hours of hip-hop dance and gymnastics at a local gym hadn't been enough to curb the underlying anger. Scott braced himself for a confrontation.

"Can we talk for a minute?" he asked.

Tamika nodded, so Scott took a seat.

"I know Chrissie sets you off." Scott referred to the petite girl with a chip on her shoulder. She'd agitated Tamika and her group since camp started. "But can I have you overlook it?"

Scott paused, waiting for an argument, but Tamika was surprisingly agreeable.

"If you can help me out, I'll try to keep Chrissie apart from you and your friends."

Tamika nodded. "I can do that."

And she did.

To Scott's amazement, the rest of camp was peaceful. After camp, a Winnie the Pooh card arrived in the mail from Tamika's caregiver, thanking the staff for camp. Tamika had included a handwritten note. "I loved it, can't wait till next year."

Scott couldn't help but smile.

Boyhood Reclaimed

"Are all church camps like this?" Juan asked Sara, a facilitator at Kearney, Nebraska, T.R.A.C. Near them, boys played football or "Ninja," a fun game mixing stealth and freeze moves.

Sara's heart broke for the 16 year old who was now about to become a father to a little girl. "This camp is extra special."

Juan's mustache twitched as Sara explained T.R.A.C.'s mission. The last rays of daylight turned to night.

"I'm doing Job Corps this fall." He outlined his plans like an adult. "And me and my girlfriend are going to church."

The two talked about faith and fatherhood.

"You know," Sara shared, "a little girl often views God based on her relationship with her dad."

Juan's eyes grew large behind his glasses as the responsibility hit him. "Wow, I never knew that."

Later, as Sara related her conversation to the staff, her eyes filled with tears. "When I found out we were from the same hometown, I put the pieces together. Juan's mother was murdered in an incident involving drugs."

Just Three Days

Will, co-director, explained how they'd made an exception for Juan's age. "He thanked us, telling us he's never done the things he got to do this weekend."

The group was quiet, musing over what three days meant to their campers. Many shouldered adult responsibilities at far too young an age. For Juan, camp not only gave him a chance to reclaim his boyhood, T.R.A.C. revealed a path of hope for him and the next generation.

Hardened

Debbie first met a hardened Jamika at the Ventura, California, Royal Family KIDS Camp. Even though the vivacious, pretty African-American girl was only a child, she acted more like a streetwise teenager than an 8 year old. She manipulated others to gain control and responded to both adults and campers with a condescending attitude.

Each year Jamika returned to camp, small changes were noticeable. By the time she graduated to T.R.A.C., Jamika emerged as a leader who made good choices. When the other girls talked about boyfriends, Jamika surprised the staff with her wisdom, especially since she had been placed in multiple foster homes.

"How are you able to make such good choices with all the bad in your life?" one of the staff asked the now 15 year old during her last year of camp.

Jamika didn't hesitate. "If it weren't for Royal Family KIDS and T.R.A.C., I wouldn't be like this."

Like Daniel, Jamika has learned God is trustworthy. Camp makes a difference.

Different Idea

After directors' training, Sandy knew how vital the challenge course was to building trust in a short period. She thought about people she knew, wondering who to ask to become the facilitators for Tyler, Texas, T.R.A.C.

When a couple from church came to mind, Sandy approached the young woman.

"My husband would be perfect," Bo agreed. "John's even certified in the low ropes course."

"Really?" Sandy knew John was athletic, but didn't know he had experience. She couldn't wait to ask John.

His answer surprised Sandy. "I don't think so." John didn't hesitate. "Been there. Done that."

Sandy tried to hide her discouragement. Apparently a low ropes program John tried to start didn't launch.

"I will pray, though," John said.

Sandy thanked him, but the doubts began to set in. *What was she thinking? How could she run a camp if she couldn't even get staff to commit?*

Six weeks later, Sandy couldn't believe her ears. Like Daniel, John prayed, and God answered.

"Count me in." John smiled. "Apparently, God had a different idea."

Part Three: Daniel and the Lions' Den

Dear Serena,

As we are completing forms for my foster girls to return to Teen Reach Adventure Camp again this summer, it seems appropriate to let you know how much your camp means to my girls. I have four girls, ages 12 to 15. Each of them is fortunate to be invited to T.R.A.C. this summer. Three of them are returning, and that seems to be even more exciting.

T.R.A.C. has been a wonderful experience for each girl. The memories of dress up, special dinners, special people and new and interesting activities have been shared with me and many others throughout the year. The wonderful photo albums help tell the stories, and the girls even show off Teen Reach pictures on their school binders all year long.

I can't even begin to comprehend the amount of time, energy and commitment needed from so many dedicated people to create this special experience. You and your staff are incredible.

I might also add that as a foster parent of four adolescent girls, I would like to say thank you for a weekend of respite. It is much appreciated.

Teen Reach is a wonderful gift that you give each foster child. Thank you for creating lifelong memories for them.

Sincerely,
J.L.

Inner Strength

"We have another one." Will's voice crackled over the two-way radio at Kearney, Nebraska, T.R.A.C. Minutes earlier a camper headed to the nurse's station because of the heat. Now Brenda complained of lightheadedness.

Angela didn't have to ask her husband what he was thinking. The two co-directors still chuckled at memories of their first girls' camp. One injury sparked a wave of sympathy pain, and T.R.A.C. nearly depleted a small town pharmacy of Ace bandages. Campers starved for love thrived on the extra attention an injury meant.

"How you feeling?" Angela asked Brenda when the golf cart rolled to a stop in front of the tan clapboard structure.

Brenda shrugged, her face flushed.

"You want to lie down? There's another bed beside the one Lizzy's using."

Nurse Audrey cared for Brenda, and Angela sat between the beds, alternately rubbing each girl's forehead. Brenda perked up and talked until it was time for the campfire and s'mores.

Saturday afternoon, Brenda loved being pampered for

the Princess Party. The dark formal she'd chosen highlighted her light blue eyes. Jason, a facilitator, handed Brenda a long-stem rose and escorted her down the red carpet into the dining room which sparkled with white lights and flickering candlelight.

After dinner, the speaker held up a paper heart. As she talked about the ways our hearts get hurt, she ripped pieces from the paper. Tears rolled down Brenda's cheeks, so her counselor, Willow, brought her to the back of the room.

"My heart's been torn like that, and I can't change the memories," Brenda confided.

Angela patted the chair beside her. She put a hand on Brenda's shoulder as they listened to Toni talk about healing a broken heart.

Low sobs racked Brenda's body, so Angela and Willow led her to the door. Overhead lights chased away the darkness as music from the dance spilled outside.

Brenda poured out her pain because her mom chose drugs over her.

"Life isn't easy," Angela agreed. "Can I share?" she mouthed to Willow, and the young counselor nodded. "It's not fair that Willow lost her husband to cancer this year." Willow teared up. "It's not easy that my husband has to be deployed next year, and my kids and I will have to say goodbye."

Brenda stopped sniffling.

Angela's eyes softened. "But life is even harder without God."

Willow agreed. "I talk to God all the time. When I'm mad, when I'm lonely, when I'm afraid."

"When God's inside you," Angela said, "He gives you a strength you don't have on your own."

Brenda wanted to pray, so Angela and Willow bowed their heads. Peace flooded Brenda's face as she asked Jesus into her heart. She returned to the dining room and danced to the Electric Slide and the Conga Line with a newfound freedom.

Later, Brenda wrote the following letter:

> I felt amazing last night. So thank you … it was the best thing ever because I accepted Christ in my heart. That was amazing how my attitude changed.
>
> Brenda

Days after camp, Willow called Angela on the phone. "For the first time since the funeral, I'm happy. T.R.A.C. helped me find a purpose again. I want to do respite care, and I'm even considering mentoring, despite the five-hour drive to Kearney."

Angela swallowed a lump in her throat. Watching God transform lives as His children put their hope in Him was nothing short of beautiful.

Sick?

Dan and Sharla first met Dylan at Royal Family KIDS when they helped with the activity center.

The kid with thick coke-bottle glasses found a Batman cape in the costume box and wore it the entire week of camp.

During a puppet show at chapel, he asked Dan if what the puppets said about heaven was true. "Are the streets really paved in gold?"

Dan nodded.

"I bet there's no pain there, either," Dylan mused. "And I bet it doesn't hurt to be a kid, either. I want to go there."

Dan swallowed the lump in his throat. "You keep reading your Bible and following Jesus, and you'll get there when it's time."

After Royal Family KIDS, Dylan attended Sherwood, Oregon, T.R.A.C. for another four years.

"This camp is sick," he told Sharla.

She furrowed her brows. "Sick?"

"Yeah, just look at the stars. They're sick. Totally cool. Awesome. Just like camp."

A smile broke out on Sharla's face. Working with teenagers, she tried to keep up with the slang, but sometimes, she lagged behind.

The young man left with his group for Cross Talk, his Bible tucked under his arm. Like Daniel, Dylan knew God could be trusted.

The Prize

"What are the prizes?" Pastor Raymond, Cross Talk teacher for The Woodlands, Texas, T.R.A.C., asked Cindy.

"Oh, no," the director explained. "The talent show isn't about competition. It's just something fun."

"You need prizes," Pastor Raymond insisted. "Or people will get mad."

"What?" Cindy exclaimed.

"Yeah. I had a dance-a-thon once, and people got mad that there weren't prizes."

"Really? What am I going to do?" Cindy hurried to find Diane, the craft and activities director. "Can you make me some kind of prize for the talent show? Something goofy or fun — it doesn't matter."

Diane agreed, so Cindy picked four random counselors to be judges. They looked daggers at her. It was obvious they didn't want to judge the kids.

The talent show proved entertaining. Acts included everything from a light show with glow sticks to singing. The blue cabin painted their faces blue like the Blue Man Group and won first place with a jazzy percussion act.

Zeke, a likeable black kid, asked for the microphone. "The blue cabin unanimously decided to award Donny first place." He handed over the last minute prize to one of the youngest campers for his amazing imitation of Michael Jackson's dance moves.

The boy, his frame severely undernourished, beamed like he'd won the world.

Later, Cindy approached the blue group. Like Daniel, they'd shown great character. "That was very thoughtful, Zeke, but I didn't see you check with your cabin."

The other boys jumped in. "He didn't have to. It was the right thing to do."

Computer Prayer Reminder

"How was girls' camp?" Jann, the church secretary, asked.

Angela, co-director of Kearney, Nebraska, T.R.A.C., shared a couple stories in the small space next to the copy machine.

"If you think to pray," she finished, "pray for Beth." It was almost a flippant comment, one said because they were in a church office.

"Beth?" Jann repeated.

"Yeah. She was one of our last minute campers. One parent is a Jew; the other practices Wiccan. I guess her parents actually provoked fighting between her and her sister."

"Wow." Jann shook her head in disbelief.

Angela nodded in agreement. It was amazing Beth's foster parent sent her to a faith-based camp. "Beth said she spent much of her life confused about religion, but after camp, she knows there is one true God."

The following year, Beth was partnered again with Linda, her counselor from before.

"Beth sees good in everyone but herself," Linda told

Angela during a break. "She moved to a new foster home in the same trailer court her dad lives, but he completely ignores her. His dismissal cuts Beth to the core."

Angela thought about the sweet-natured girl whose modesty was evident in both her choice of swimwear and the elegant cream-colored gown she had chosen for the formal night. Beth's picture at the gazebo stood out among the others. No one would believe the pain she carried inside.

Camp ended, and Angela found herself back in the church office, talking with Jann, the circumstances so similar; it was almost déjà vu.

"Did Beth come back?" Jann asked, expectation written on her face.

Angela was surprised Jann remembered Beth's name. "She made a pact with Linda to read the Bible this next year."

"Good." Jann smiled. "I've been praying for her. Every day, my computer flashed a reminder."

"Really?" Angela felt convicted. *Would she ever have the faith of Daniel?*

The same Father who prompted Jann to pray has great plans for Beth.

Part Three: Daniel and the Lions' Den

Dear T.R.A.C.,

Thank you for having me at T.R.A.C. this year! It was so much fun! At camp I learned that God knows how many strands of hair you have and how many times you sit down and get up. I made many new friends here, and they are all amazing, beautiful people. My favorite part of camp was getting to be a princess for a while and learning how to ride a horse. I can't wait to see you next year!

Jordan

Does God Still Love Me?

Campers hummed along to an Evanescence song which played during Cross Talk at Scio, Oregon, T.R.A.C.

"Feel free to highlight any words that speak to you," Terresa invited the girls. Permanent markers waited next to a poster of the song lyrics.

Teressa's daughter and a facilitator was the first to stand. She circled the word father and crossed it out repeatedly. Her vulnerability opened dialogue with the entire group.

"Why do people cut?" a camper wanted to know.

"Why do boys want to have sex with me?" another girl asked.

"Great questions," Terresa encouraged the girls. "God can turn what was meant for evil into greater good." Compassion filled her eyes. "No topic is off limits at camp. There's nothing you can't ask us."

A camper named Taylor cleared her throat. "Does God still love me even if I'm bisexual?"

Terresa met her gaze. Her earlier nervousness at teaching Cross Talk for the first time disappeared as she felt God's spirit flood her. "God loves you, Taylor. While we were yet sinners, He died for us."

Part Three: Daniel and the Lions' Den

Terresa pointed to scripture after scripture.

Later that evening, Terresa asked for volunteers to act out the story of Daniel. Several hands shot up. The "lions" donned manes made from felt strips and "Daniel" wore a shepherd's tunic.

Applause broke out when "Daniel" emerged from the den unharmed.

"Now, we're going to change things up a bit," Terresa said. "What if Daniel lived in our world today, facing a different kind of lion?" Confused expressions dotted the audience.

"Here's a baseball cap, Daniel." Terresa put a cap backward on a camper's head. "You're in the hood, and your 'lions' are hood rats."

The "lions" flipped their manes over. On the underside, big words written in glitter showed on the felt strips. "Sex, drugs, alcohol, cutting."

The girls watched in rapt attention.

"Daniel faced lions that would eat him. Today's lions — sex with multiple partners, drugs, alcohol, cutting — will kill you in a different way." Terresa paused, letting the words linger. "What is your lion?"

Taylor's eyes locked on Terresa. Bisexuality was her lion. Hiding it was killing her inside.

Will God still love me?

The earlier question lingered in their unspoken conversation.

Yes, Taylor, He does. And God is bigger than the lions.

Writing on a T.R.A.C. T-shirt

Tim, director of Omaha, Nebraska, T.R.A.C., noticed Colby's red eyes, so he took a seat next to the young man on the two-hour bus ride home.

"You okay?"

Colby shook his head. "I had dreams of my dad coming after me with knives again."

Tim sighed, wondering what he could say. Even though Colby had been adopted, painful memories still lingered. "Was my first year at Royal Family KIDS the first time you'd been to camp?"

Colby shrugged. "I don't remember."

"Well, I remember you." Tim grinned. "You had the top bunk on the left side next to the bathroom."

"How'd you remember that?"

"You made a big impression on me," Tim answered.

Colby's eyes lit up. "Really?"

Tim nodded. "You're one of the reasons I got involved with T.R.A.C."

The following day, Tim received a message from Colby. "I'm thinking about donating some of my own money to T.R.A.C. ... I really appreciate the camp and everyone at it. P.S. I'm praying for you, and I'm trying to read the whole Bible. I like Psalm 13, 23 and 24. Read them, even though you probably already have."

Tim couldn't help but grin at the smiley face.

"After this year, I decided with the love of the people around me that I need the Lord in my life ... After I got home from camp, I prayed for Jesus to be in my life and lead me ... and to help me read the whole Bible so I can grow to be a godly man as someone said on the back of my T.R.A.C. shirt. Thank you."

Tim wiped a tear from his eye. Colby's desire to be a godly man like Daniel grew from Royal Family KIDS and T.R.A.C.

Golden Rule Marble

Michael, co-founder of Arizona's Hope & A Future, rolled the marble he'd kept all these years in his palm. The metallic sheen glinted in the light. Imprinted on a gold band around the circumference was the Golden Rule, a verse Michael's grandmother quoted often. "Do unto others as you would have them do unto you."

The marble would make a great gift for campers. After all, Michael had received the marble at summer camp when he was 12 or 13, and like Daniel, his relationship with God had developed over the years.

The founder of Samsonite originally shared the core value of his company by giving away the marbles, and Michael wanted to pass on the same legacy. He purchased several marbles online before they went out of production. Now campers receive yellow wristbands instead, which read, "Live the Golden Rule."

When a resolution designating Arizona as a "Golden Rule State" came across the desk of Michael's mother, Arizona Secretary of State Jan Brewer, she signed it, creating a program for nominating people who exemplified the Golden Rule.

Now governor, she's presented Golden Rule Citizen

certificates to both Royal Family KIDS and T.R.A.C. volunteers.

Campers and staff are in good company.

President Bush received a Golden Rule marble when Michael attended a White House function. Then Michael gave one of his last marbles to President Obama when he came to Tucson, and the moment was captured on C-SPAN.

A simple token inscribed with a treasured rule rests in the hands of both campers and presidents.

Part Four
Gutsy Conversations:
Jonah and the Whale

First-year campers often arrive at T.R.A.C. convinced three days in the outdoors is stupid. They stand on the perimeter, angry and withdrawn. A few attempt to run. Many have rejected God. Others have perpetuated the cycle of abuse and become abusers themselves.

At camp, teens hear God pursues us, even when, like Jonah, we reject Him. God sent a great fish to swallow Jonah before he could drown in his problems. Foster teens can identify, often knowing the same despair. They come to T.R.A.C. with no hope the future will be different and learn Psalm 120:1, which reads, "I call on the Lord in my distress, and He answers me." As many foster teens have discovered through T.R.A.C., God hears our cries — even from the belly of the fish — and He is merciful.

Miracle at the Fishing Hole

Ask Serena, co-founder of T.R.A.C., a fishing story, and one immediately comes to mind.

Max stood along the bank of the fishing hole with the other campers in his group. Green-blue water reflected puffy white clouds as Serena's father gave a casting lesson.

"Cast your line into the water like this," he said, showing the group what he meant.

The hook hit the surface, and Serena's father immediately landed a huge trout.

"It's a miracle!" Max exclaimed. He was a small kid with jet black hair and pale skin, looking much younger than his 12 years.

The older man's wrinkles creased into a smile. He didn't tell Max the fish stocked in the pond hadn't been fed in three days.

Max could hardly wait to tell Serena. As soon as the group finished fishing, he hurried along the gravel road back to the lodge. "Serena!" a ruddy-faced Max called out. "There was a miracle at the fishing hole."

"Yeah?"

Max talked so fast, he tripped over his words. "There

wasn't even a worm on that hook. And he caught a salmon."

"A salmon?" Serena thought about the fish they'd stocked. "It's probably a trout."

Max shook his head. "No, I'm sure it was a salmon." He beamed. "You gotta tell everybody. Tell them there was a miracle at the fishing hole."

Repentance

Janey came to girls' T.R.A.C. at Sherwood, Oregon, as a high-risk sex offender.

Unlike other camps, T.R.A.C. could accept Janey because of strict adherence to safety measures like the "two-deep" rule, which leaves no room for the abused to become an abuser.

The girl with the long blond hair quickly emerged as a strong leader with a sweet, tender heart.

"I wish I could hug you," she told Serena at the end of T.R.A.C.

"I know." Serena felt the same longing, but Child Protective Services established firm rules to govern Janey's behavior.

"I really appreciate you letting me come to camp," Janey confided. "Thanks for giving me a chance."

"Don't forget what we learned at Cross Talk," Serena reminded her. "Think about repentance. That was a message for you. You can't continue in your behavior."

The second year at camp, Janey decided to accept Christ into her heart, and a staff member volunteered to be her mentor.

Watching Janey thrive in this relationship birthed T.R.A.C.*life*, a mentoring program for campers.

Now Janey is married, and the first in her family to attend college. T.R.A.C. continues to be close to her heart as the place where she discovered a future beyond the belly of despair.

Part Four: Jonah and the Whale

Dear Serena and Tim,

I really appreciated it when you let me come to your camp. It was the best experience of my life! I appreciate that you care so much about foster kids. I really enjoyed all of the fun things we did.

The fishing was so fun. I thought it was cool that I caught a fish right at the end. When we went to the challenge course, it was very exciting and interesting. I think that gaining trust in people is good, and it is very hard for me. I loved the horseback riding because I love horses. The activity center was fun, too, and there were a lot of people to help us with our projects.

I enjoyed all the great things you gave us. The Bible is so cool. I read it every day during my free time. I hope that I will finish it before next year. I pray every night before I go to sleep.

The shirt is neat. I will always keep it. I also loved the T.R.A.C. backpack that you gave us.

The luau on Saturday was so fun, getting our hair and makeup done, plus Hawaiian food. It was all so good. YUM!

Serena, I was so grateful that you trusted me to come to your camp. It felt good to have you trust me. On the last day when I said goodbye to you, I was so happy when you asked me to come back next year. That felt really good.

Janey

The Label

Surianne came to Manhattan, Kansas, T.R.A.C. with a "no run court order." One more run and she'd be placed in juvenile detention.

Fear prickled Michelle's skin when Lisa, the co-director, asked her to be Surianne's counselor. *What kind of problems would this girl cause? Would she run like Jonah?*

"What's her name?" Michelle asked.

"Surianne."

The unusual name sparked recognition. Michelle knew Surianne; she attended the high school where Michelle worked.

At camp, the two connected instantly. Surianne was never a problem. In fact, she'd only run from a bad placement. Surianne had been in her current foster home for eight months without any issues.

Labels often follow kids in the foster system. T.R.A.C. goes beyond the label.

Skipping Stones

Trevor lobbed a stone across the stream at Scio, Oregon, T.R.A.C. It skipped multiple times before sinking.

In contrast, Terresa's stone sank immediately to the bottom.

Trevor tossed another rock which nearly reached the other side.

"Look at you," the Cross Talk teacher praised him. "You're good at this."

A smile crossed the face of the skinny young man with black hair. "You know, I didn't even want to come to camp."

"Yeah?" Terresa listened.

He nodded. "Thanks for sharing your stories. It makes me realize God's been helping me this whole time."

Terresa nodded. "God wanted you at camp."

Trevor fingered a stone. "I didn't know I was so strong, but God's given me strength to walk through things with my stepfather."

"Like the verse we've been learning about Jonah," Terresa agreed. "I call on the Lord in my distress, and He answers me."

Silence settled around them.

Just Three Days

Trevor flicked his wrist, and a large rock jumped across the surface. It rippled the water just like the truth which touched Trevor.

Part Four: Jonah and the Whale

Dear T.R.A.C.,

My foster daughter needs a lot of love and encouragement. Katie often has a hard time fitting in and has a difficult time keeping friends. I know a lot of love and encouragement was poured into her during camp. Katie has a difficult life, and I am grateful to you for taking the time to speak life and love into this hurting young lady. She has been able to express herself without feeling judged.

Thanks!
L.B.

Psalm 82:3

Gary, Cross Talk teacher at Glendale, Arizona, T.R.A.C., looked across his audience at boys' camp.

Few owned a Bible, so he began to explain the division between the Old and New Testaments and the various books.

As the boys studied the table of contents, Gary asked for someone to call out a book.

"Psalms," a camper answered.

"How about a chapter number?"

"Eighty-two," a different young man shot out.

"And a verse."

"Three," a third camper spoke up.

Gary had their attention so he decided to move into the story of Jonah.

He didn't take the time to look up the verse in Psalms, and no one asked.

That night, Michael, a counselor and co-founder of Arizona's Hope & A Future, took off his name badge and saw the scripture reference in Psalms. When he opened his Bible, he nearly fell out of his chair. Michael couldn't believe what he read.

Part Four: Jonah and the Whale

"You're not going to believe this." Michael called the staff over the two-way radios. Static crackled in his ear. "Listen to Psalm 82:3."

Michael read, "Defend the cause of the weak and fatherless; maintain the rights of the poor and oppressed."

The staff was equally dumbfounded. *What were the odds? The book and numbers were random, yet the verse perfectly described the mission of T.R.A.C.*

The same God who pursued Jonah reminded the Glendale staff the teens at T.R.A.C. are close to His heart.

Camp Caretaker

"Thanks for everything." Cindy, director of The Woodlands, Texas, T.R.A.C., returned the campground keys to Phil, the caretaker. "The kids had a great time."

"Your kids aren't foster kids." Phil shook his head.

Cindy hid her surprise.

"Yes, they are."

"No, they're not," Phil insisted. "I know foster kids." The campground was owned by an adoption and foster care placement agency, so Phil was familiar with camps run for state wards.

"But they are," Cindy tried to convince the caretaker. "T.R.A.C. has kids on probation. Several come from detention centers."

Phil wasn't buying it. "I see foster kids come here throughout the year. And I never see you restraining kids or holding them down."

"What?" Cindy exclaimed. "What do you mean?"

"Your staff's not burnt out. The kids don't have issues."

How could Cindy explain the difference? The small camper-to-adult ratio at T.R.A.C. allowed support for campers with major medical and behavioral issues, but there was so much more. God showed up at T.R.A.C. He wanted teens to know His love. There was hope beyond the belly of despair.

"See you next year, Phil." Cindy grinned. She didn't need to say anything.

Love spoke clearly.

Camp Sucks!

Sixteen disgruntled teenagers lined up for pictures at registration for Scio, Oregon, T.R.A.C. They grumbled like Jonah. No one smiled.

The 30-minute van ride to camp was no better. The boys slumped in their seats. Their body language shouted, "Camp sucks! Is it over yet?"

At the end of three days, staff sorted through pictures from camp.

Boys fishing.

Campers hunting for crawdads.

Friends canoeing.

Cabin groups playing games.

Smiles shone from every picture. In stark contrast, the earlier registration photos looked like mug shots from jail.

What was the real difference between the two stacks of photos?

Hope shone from the faces after T.R.A.C.

The Accident

"Camp would be so good for Casey," the therapist told Tim, co-director of Sherwood, Oregon, T.R.A.C., over the phone.

Tim listened to the description of the young sexual offender. His heart hurt for the boy with a history of sexual abuse. Casey's mother, a stripper and prostitute, brought men home. The boy endured much abuse until he found safety in a closet where he stayed for hours.

"You have to know, Casey's never made it through anything," the therapist confided in Tim. "He implodes after about three hours."

Tim arranged for Casey to attend camp. If God pursued Jonah, He would pursue Casey. Besides most kids labeled "bad kids" wanted nothing more than to be a "normal kid." After prayer and conferring with Serena, Tim asked a longtime Royal Family KIDS volunteer to work one-on-one as Casey's counselor. Billy immediately agreed.

At camp, Casey instantly bonded with Billy, a 70-year-old retired beat cop whose son had been killed on police duty in a gang situation. At lunch, Casey had a question.

"Why do you treat me so nice?"

Billy didn't hesitate. "Because that's how I treated my own sons, and that's how I want to treat you."

Casey couldn't believe it. He'd never known the love of either his father or grandfather.

In woodworking, Casey built a bi-winged plane which he painted red. He carried it everywhere he went at camp.

Saturday morning at breakfast, Tim told the boys a surprise waited later that day. The excitement built as staff passed out prayer cards.

Tim read his card of encouragement at the same table where Billy and Casey sat.

Casey turned over his card. "Who's this Mackenzie?"

"Mackenzie who?" Tim asked absently.

"Mackenzie Howell."

Tim's eyes widened. "Mackenzie's my daughter."

"God loves you a lot," Casey began to read. "I hope you have a wonderful time at camp. I'm praying for you. And I love you."

Casey asked her age. "Four," Tim answered.

"Why would your daughter pray for a guy like me?" Casey stared at Tim with piercing eyes. Longing mixed with regret. "She doesn't know the awful things I've done." A tear slipped down his face.

"Because this camp is about God's love." Tim and Billy wiped watery eyes. "And second chances."

Later that morning, Tim got the awful call that there'd been an accident. He jumped in his truck and headed down the road. Not far away, a track hoe lay on its side in the ditch.

"The trailer gave out." Tim's friend Richard was distraught. "The track hoe flipped over."

"I'm so sorry." Tim shook his head, imagining how much damage the machine sustained. He hated to disappoint the campers. The surprise was ruined. They couldn't help operate the track hoe with Richard later.

"This is my dad's machine." Richard was beside himself. "A wreck like this will ruin the engine."

Tim exhaled. "I'm so sorry, Richard. We'll help with whatever."

"I got a guy coming to help me," Richard said. "I wish things were different."

Tim didn't want to leave, but he was needed back at camp. "I need to help with lunch. Then I'll be back. I'll have the boys pray." The words seemed almost trite as Tim left Richard on the side of the road with the wreck.

"Boys," Tim addressed the campers a half hour later, "I'm really sorry, but the surprise we planned for later can't happen."

Shoulders sagged and disappointment echoed through the crowd as Tim explained. He hoped the boys wouldn't see the incident as one more broken promise.

"Would anyone like to pray for Richard and the track hoe?" he asked.

A hand rose at the back. When Casey stood up, Tim tried to hide his shock.

"God," Casey prayed earnestly, "Richard was trying to

help us kids. Would You do a miracle?"

The prayer of faith uttered by a kid without faith left Tim dumbfounded.

A year later, Casey rushed off the bus and made a beeline to Tim. "What happened to the track hoe?"

Tim grinned. "Nothing. The engine worked perfectly. The mechanics couldn't figure it out."

Casey's jaw dropped. "I can't believe it. God heard my prayer." He looked at Tim. "I've been reading my Bible every day. I guess God really does exist."

After camp, the therapist confirmed what Tim already knew. T.R.A.C. changed Casey. Three days brought Casey from heartbreak to hope.

The Cross

"Look!" A camper pointed, and heads turned upward at Kearney, Nebraska, T.R.A.C. Two jets crossed above, their contrails leaving a huge white cross in the sky.

"Cool! A cross!" The girls, listening to the story of Jonah, were visibly impressed. The timing couldn't be more perfect.

Daylight faded, turning the lake water inky black. The cross lingered in the sky. The same God who sent a big fish to save Jonah painted a picture of His love to a handful of girls at a Midwest camp set in a sea of cornfields.

Big Boy

What're we gonna do with this big boy?

Tim, T.R.A.C. director of Omaha, Nebraska, didn't voice his intimidation as the 15-year-old linebacker walked off the bus.

Tyson, nicknamed Ty, and his siblings came to live with family in Omaha after his mother was imprisoned. It wasn't long before the kids ended up in foster care.

At camp, Ty quickly became a favorite with everyone. The staff fell in love with his big heart. Campers responded to his leadership. Ty embraced everything, jumping into singing and helping lead worship. He even broke up a fight between two kids at the lake before a counselor intervened.

On the bus ride home, Ty sat next to Mark, Royal Family KIDS director for Omaha and T.R.A.C. volunteer.

"I've seen the way men live their lives at camp," Ty told Mark. "And I really got to thinking about who I'm hanging with every day. I'm a leader, but I haven't been the right kind of leader. Not like at camp. I need to be a positive leader back home."

Part Four: Jonah and the Whale

Not long after, Ty moved back to Louisiana. Mark and Tim don't know the rest of Ty's story, but they trust God. Three days changed Jonah. And three days impacted Ty.

Just Three Days

Dear T.R.A.C.,

Thank you for showing me the right way to God — the way that I would never have found. Thank you for letting me and everyone else have fun, and you helped me make new friends. My life has been really hard. I barely get to see my brother and sisters.

Julio

Part Four: Jonah and the Whale

The Hug

"Just one more, Gary," Jeno repeated in his typical monosyllabic tone. "One more, Gary." Purple-black juice stained his fingertips and lips.

Gary, facilitator at Scio, Oregon, T.R.A.C., steadied the canoe under the overhanging blackberry vines. Water lapped against the aluminum sides while Jeno reached for another handful of berries. A canoe of boys rowed past them, their laughter carrying across the water.

"Just one more, Gary."

Gary smiled at Jeno's innocence. The autistic boy who recoiled from touch quickly warmed up to Gary. When Jeno got off the bus the first day of camp, he wouldn't look anyone in the eye and backed away when Gary tried to give him a safe side hug.

"Those motorcycle guys were cool, Gary." Jeno recited the names of the six bikers who roared into camp earlier in the day.

"You are amazing," Gary marveled. Despite being almost blind in one eye, Jeno had a photographic memory.

Jeno named the make and model of each motorcycle as the two spent a lazy afternoon under the blackberry vines.

Later, when the campers loaded into the vans, Gary

found his buddy. "Hey, Jeno, how are you? Did you have fun at camp?"

The boy with the short-cropped hair and bad teeth grinned back.

"Do you want a hug?"

Jeno nodded, venturing from his belly of fear. This time he didn't back away.

Silver Coins

The campers at Royal Family KIDS called him Damian, the demon, because he was so mean and angry to everyone around him. By the time he came to Sherwood, Oregon, T.R.A.C., Damian was broken and withdrawn. No one messed with Damian; one spark would set him off.

Mike, a volunteer, hid $50 in silver coins around camp. Damian and the other campers ran around the woods, hunting for silver with Mike's metal detector. The campers could keep the silver or use the money at the T.R.A.C. store to buy things for themselves, but Damian had a different idea.

At the awards ceremony on the last day of camp, Damian wanted to make a presentation.

"Would you come forward, Tim and Serena?" he asked.

"You've done so much for us," Damian told them in front of the other campers and staff. "We can't say thank you enough for starting T.R.A.C. Because of what you've done, kids like us can come to camp."

He presented Tim and Serena with a box of silver coins. "We want to give you our silver coins, so you can start more camps."

Just Three Days

Tim and Serena were overcome with emotion. Despite hardships, these teens who had nothing gave everything.

"Because of your act of charity," Tim told Damian, "I will use your story to raise thousands of dollars so that other teens in foster care can attend Teen Reach Adventure Camp."

Part Four: Jonah and the Whale

Last Minute Camper

"Can Jonathon go to camp with my other foster boys?" the woman asked at the registration table. Of all the foster families Cindy had worked with since becoming The Woodlands, Texas, T.R.A.C. director three years earlier, this woman caused Cindy the most concern. She struggled to meet the needs of the large brood under her care.

Cindy scanned the faces before her, and a familiar ache throbbed in her chest. She never imagined falling in love with so many teens; Cindy could almost feel God swelling her heart three times its size. No way could she turn away a camper.

"Fill out his information." Cindy handed a camper application to the woman. She smiled at Jonathon who grinned back.

Jonathon's lighthearted personality made him a popular fit with the boys in the yellow cabin. In fact, the entire yellow cabin, most of whom were two- and three-year veterans of T.R.A.C., knew how the staff adored them and quickly let their familiarity cause problems. They were wild and rowdy, throwing around their weight like they owned camp. The boys interrupted Cross Talk and flirted with the female staff.

"What are we going to do with the yellow cabin?" exhausted counselors asked Cindy during a meeting on the first night of camp.

"We couldn't complete one challenge," the facilitators jumped in. "The boys kept interrupting us to tell jokes and impress each other."

"Let's pray." Cindy bowed her head and soon felt led to talk to the boys about respect.

The next day, before any activities, Cindy and Raymond, the Cross Talk teacher, went to the yellow cabin.

"Good morning, boys," Cindy greeted the group. "Care if we chat?"

Talking to the group proved to be an exercise in futility. Jonathon would cut up, and the others would laugh or another camper would make a face. Cindy couldn't get in one sentence without someone interrupting. Raymond, the Cross Talk teacher, mirrored her frustration.

"This is why I need to talk to you boys." Cindy's exasperation finally quieted them. "I can't even get in three words because you keep interrupting." Her chest rose as she looked each one in the eye. "I don't believe this is your heart. But you're being disrespectful. And as leaders at camp, you have a huge responsibility to the younger campers. They look up to you and want to be in the yellow cabin."

"She's right," an athletic kid nicknamed Stretch agreed.

Part Four: Jonah and the Whale

He was the quarterback on his high school football team and made excellent grades. "We are leaders."

"Yeah," another one of the boys piped up. "We're like the role models here."

Realization shone in the eyes of a tall, thin kid named Ben. He'd been allowed to come to camp after Cindy talked to his probation officer concerning his trouble with drugs. Until this point, Cindy wondered if Ben had ever considered himself a leader.

"Cindy," Stretch proclaimed in a deep voice, "from now on, you're going to see a difference."

"Good." Cindy smiled, though she had her doubts. She'd raised two teenagers and watched many conversations go through one ear and out the other.

"You know I'm older," Raymond spoke up. "And I lose my train of thought easily. Could you also help me at Cross Talk by not interrupting?"

The boys apologized.

By Saturday night, the staff was dumbfounded. "Who are these guys? Someone in the yellow cabin messes up, and the rest of the group corrects him." Campers noticed, too.

One concern, however, remained. The boys still flirted with the female staff and tried to wrap their arms around them. One boy even kissed a staff member on the cheek.

As the staff shared their concerns during the meeting, one of the boys from the yellow cabin and two staff members approached.

"Hey, there," Cindy addressed the camper. "We have a problem. The ladies are feeling like they aren't being respected."

He shrugged, making Cindy wonder what impact her words had.

Back in the cabin, however, the young man burst into the room. "Guys, we have to talk about a problem."

Later, Kevin, one of the "night angels," a staff member who relieved the counselors for some downtime, reported the conversation to Cindy.

"I've never witnessed anything like it," he told Cindy. "The guys started talking about their inappropriate behavior with the female staff, and pretty soon, Jonathon admitted his girlfriend was pregnant."

"Well, what are you going to do?" someone asked Jonathon. "Step up and be a father or walk out of his life?"

One after another, the boys shared deep wounds from their own fathers. Kevin, barely able to contain the flood of emotions rolling over him, suggested prayer. "Why don't we pray about Jonathon's decision before bed?"

"Why not pray right now?" Joey, a soft-spoken kid who carried a lot of pain, piped up.

The boys gathered in a circle and presented heartfelt concerns to the Father. Like Jonah, they were learning they could cry out to Him and He would never leave them.

"It was the most amazing transformation I've ever witnessed." Kevin choked up when he told Cindy. "The boys turned into young men before my eyes. Their requests were uttered in all seriousness with a complete reliance on God. Jonathon started weeping, and the boys rallied around him, asking God to help him be a father to his kid."

Tears filled Cindy's eyes. She could hardly believe the change. Somewhere a little baby's life would be different because God brought a last minute camper.

A Furry Angel

Thick black eyeliner ringed brooding eyes. All-black Goth clothing shouted, "Stay away!"

Angela, co-director of Kearney, Nebraska, T.R.A.C., saw the girl riding her bicycle in the neighborhood and tried to remember why she looked familiar. Tasha had come to church with a friend from Royal Family KIDS, but stopped coming when she was admitted to the mental health hospital.

Camp was a month away, and three spots remained open, so Angela e-mailed Prairie, the camp behavioral specialist, who worked at the same hospital. She asked Prairie if she could get a camp application to Tasha, but the girl was no longer a client.

"God," Angela prayed, "fill these spots with the girls You want."

A few days later, Angela's Chihuahua-terrier mix escaped from the backyard. A woman called to let her know she had Izzy. The address was not far from her home. "Are you the person I talked with?" Angela asked a woman with glasses sitting in the garage.

"Bring out the dog!" the woman yelled toward a door. "The owners are here."

Part Four: Jonah and the Whale

Angela nearly fell over when Tasha walked out with Izzy. *What were the odds Izzy would end up here?* Angela didn't even know where Tasha lived. She mentioned T.R.A.C., and Tasha's mother wanted two applications — one for Tasha and another for a cousin with a troubled past. Both girls attended camp the following month.

"That's amazing," Angela marveled to her daughters as they walked home. "Izzy was an angel today."

"Did she fly?" Keely lit up.

Meghan laughed at her little sister, but doubt crossed her face.

"No." Angela smiled. The same God who used a big fish in Jonah's life could use a little dog. "God answers prayers. Even if He has to use a puppy."

Blindfold

"I'm not doing the minefield," Alexiis refused on the challenge course at Spokane, Washington. "I hate blindfolds."

Hot tears burned Terresa's eyes. She and her daughter were together at facilitator training for Scio, Oregon, T.R.A.C. The others in the group couldn't understand the depth of painful memories mother and daughter associated with blindfolds.

Even Terresa, a victim of spousal abuse for 17 years, didn't realize the abuse her daughter endured from her stepfather until the details emerged during divorce proceedings. The thought still made her stomach revolt.

Alexiis stood back while her mother participated in the minefield challenge. Terresa guided another trainee through a maze of debris while the rest of the group circled them, screaming in an attempt to steer the blindfolded trainee off course.

Frustration rose in Terresa. *How often had she listened to the same voices screaming for her attention rather than the still, small voice of God, leading her through the minefield of life?* Terresa could empathize with the campers on a whole new level. The challenge made mother and daughter confront the past. *How many campers would experience the same?*

After refusing to participate in challenges for two days, Alexiis finally agreed to the trust fall.

The group cheered in support. Bonding together had increased their transparency.

"I'm just gonna do it." Alexiis clenched her teeth. "You better be here, God. Now."

Terresa watched as her daughter fell back into the arms of the group. A grin erupted on Alexiis' face when the group caught her. Applause rang out.

Alexiis jumped out of their arms and into her mother's embrace. For years they'd sat in the pews at church, never letting anyone inside their hurt. But that changed on a challenge course when the two finally let go. And now God would use them to help others trapped in the same belly of pain.

Half-Court Shot

Clay refused to participate in the challenge course. Like Jonah, he grumbled at God.

"Betcha can't make a layup?" Aimee challenged the Native American camper who could've been a linebacker. She and Kori, staff members at Glendale, Arizona, T.R.A.C., shot baskets with him on the court.

Clay made the shot with ease.

Aimee and Kori took a turn, but Clay cut them down with derogatory comments. The mean streak prevented others from getting too close.

"We know you're joking." Aimee laughed, ignoring the comments. "You don't mean that."

"What about here?" Kori challenged Clay from a spot farther from the basket. "Can you make it from here?"

The ball swished through the net.

The ladies cheered. Slowly, the hand Clay used to protect his neck remained down for longer than just the moment he took a shot. Aimee wondered if he'd ever been strangled. She knew Clay and his brothers had been split up and taken from an alcoholic, abusive background.

"Watch me make it from half court," Clay bragged. He aimed and missed.

Part Four: Jonah and the Whale

"Good try." Kori clapped.

Clay attempted the shot again.

And again.

And again.

The ladies never wavered in their applause, and Clay never quit. Sweat trickled down his face until he finally sank the ball.

"Yes!" He lifted his arms in victory.

"You did it." Kori and Clay slapped high fives. "You have amazing determination. I bet you can focus on anything you set your mind to — school, whatever."

Clay grinned. "Race you back," he challenged and took off.

"Hey, wait," Kori called out.

"Hurry." Aimee encouraged Kori to catch up.

Clay won.

The shell cracked, and Clay had fun the rest of camp.

Connection

Scott, director of Kitsap County, Washington, T.R.A.C., knew the quiet teen with the lisp from the junior high where he taught. School was a challenge for Philip, who had an individualized education plan, but none of his differences showed up at camp. Without the normal peer pressure, Philip had a great time.

After camp, Scott and his family seemed to run into Philip everywhere — Costco, the ferry, the marina. Each time, Philip's face lit up. The chance encounters cemented the connection made at camp, reminding Philip that life doesn't have to be lived in the belly of despair. The future can be different.

Advice from a Teen Mom

E-mail drafted, Angela, co-director of Kearney, Nebraska, T.R.A.C., hit send. Ryan had a huge heart for the foster kids he placed with Christian families through Compass, a private group which contracted with state health and human services. With two spots left at girls' camp, Angela wondered if Ryan had any teens who would qualify.

"Sherry's had her baby," he wrote back. "Do you want me to ask her about camp?"

Angela cringed. Teens got enough wrong messages from movies like *Juno* and the MTV show *Teen Mom*. Camp was supposed to be a safe haven; not one more place to send the message that teen motherhood was a good thing.

"Does the baby live with her?" she asked Ryan.

"No, the state took her son, but Sherry's trying hard to change so she can get him back."

Angela thought about the Princess Party with its focus on purity.

"Sherry's been in a couple different homes this past year. She's had a lot of issues," Ryan continued. "Since the birth, Sherry's been more open spiritually."

Angela promised to get back to Ryan and then breathed a prayer for wisdom and direction.

A couple days later, a woman called about a boy in her group home. "I know it's late, but do you have any openings left? Jim would love to go to camp."

When Jim's application arrived, Angela looked at his picture in disbelief. Jim and his sister had come to church when a friend invited them. Months passed, and Angela hadn't seen either one. The woman at the group home promised to pass along an application to Jim's sister, Jada.

Angela got a call a few days later from Jada, age 15. "Did you know I had a baby girl?"

She tried not to stutter. "Oh, yeah, what's her name?"

"Josie."

Angela had the answer for Ryan. Sherry and Jada could be partners at camp.

A month later, the campers stood in a circle for the opening icebreaker. Sherry stood on a paper plate in the center and called out, "I want to share common ground with anyone who's had a kid."

Angela and her husband, Will, exchanged a look. *So much for keeping the young moms under the radar.* The girls hadn't even been at camp for 30 minutes; what did the next few days hold?

Both Sherry and Jada loved camp. Smiles lit up their faces while jumping on the water trampoline, doing crafts and petting the horses.

For three days, the clock rewound, and they were

young girls again, not teen moms loaded with the responsibility of infants.

Another camper, Cassie, age 12, was obsessed with babies. She had tons of questions for both Sherry and Jada.

Their counselor, Rosemary, started to discourage the conversation until she heard the response.

"Don't do it," Sherry told Cassie.

"Yeah," agreed Jada. "Being a teen mom isn't like what's on TV. It's hard work."

Cassie listened intently. By the end of camp, she seemed convinced teen motherhood was not everything she believed.

After camp, Angela e-mailed Ryan to tell him the positive difference Sherry made in Cassie's life. Apparently T.R.A.C. had an equal impact on Sherry. Before camp, she complained on Facebook about going to a lame Christian camp; after camp, she couldn't say enough good about T.R.A.C. Three days — like Jonah's time in the fish — turned Sherry's attitude 180 degrees.

Broken Arm

The night before campers arrived at Sherwood, Oregon, T.R.A.C., Lily fell on her arm while she and the other counselors decorated the tents. A trip to the hospital revealed a break.

Lily felt awful, but Sharla reassured her God would provide another counselor.

Sharla whispered a prayer as she looked through her list of potential staff and dialed a number. She believed Psalm 120:1, which reads, "I call on the Lord in my distress, and He answers me."

Colleen's response gave Sharla goose bumps. "I was just asking God what He wanted me to do this weekend," Colleen said. "I guess I'm coming to camp."

Chance Meeting

Sunday afternoons usually meant naptime for Ted, who'd been a counselor at Scio, Oregon, T.R.A.C., but this Sunday in May, he felt an urge to ride a 10-mile loop in the country.

He hadn't done much physical activity since he hurt his ankle the winter after camp, so the desire was a bit unusual.

Ted enjoyed the solitude as he passed several farmhouses. At one, a box rested next to several dozen fresh eggs. The honor system made Ted smile. Being in the middle of nowhere had its advantages.

Past a swale, Ted came upon a kid holding a fishing pole. They were miles from a place to fish, so this seemed odd. Another kid wearing a skateboard helmet sat alongside a bike several hundred feet away.

"Peter?" Ted didn't hide the surprise in his voice.

"Ted?" The lanky dark-haired kid hadn't changed much physically since Ted had been his counselor at T.R.A.C.

"What are you doing out here?" Ted didn't know much about Peter's history, except that Peter didn't care if he ever saw his dad again.

"Been fishing. We're headed home." Peter and his friend had been walking for hours.

Ted and Peter reminisced about camp, and Ted asked Peter about school and wrestling.

"I've already been practicing." Peter lit up when Ted remembered his love for the sport. "I can't wait till the season starts."

Peter played it cool around his friend, but Ted sensed the undercurrent of excitement over their shared memories.

When they parted, Ted had to shake his head. God had a divine appointment for him that day. Peter needed a reminder God still heard when he called.

During wrestling season, Ted scanned the match results in the newspaper. Peter's name was never listed, so Ted wondered if he moved to another foster family.

Ted continues to bike the same route he met Peter on that spring Sunday. Each time he nears the concrete bridge, he prays, knowing God has not forgotten Peter.

Part Four: Jonah and the Whale

Dear T.R.A.C.,

Camp has had a huge impact on my foster son. He so looks forward to attending each year and is excited about the possibility of being a camp leader one day. He was so excited to attend camp again to show how much he had improved from the prior year. My foster son has a strong desire to do well, and T.R.A.C. is a place where he can do that.

Thank you!
P.T.

The Runner

Leslie packed her bags at Kitsap County, Washington, T.R.A.C. and took off down the beach. She made it a hundred yards before she gave up and plopped down in the sand.

Scott, the director, sat beside Leslie. The behavior specialist stayed back, waiting to intervene if necessary.

Silence stretched between the two.

"So, you going to say something?" Leslie finally spoke up after 20 minutes.

"Why'd you run?" Scott asked.

Life had already hardened Leslie's pleasant features. "I told you I want to go home."

Scott reminded Leslie that her caregiver refused. "She thinks camp will be good for you."

Leslie tightened her fists. They talked until Scott persuaded Leslie to rejoin the others.

The following year, Leslie returned to camp. Her counselor, Cheri, reluctantly agreed to be paired with Leslie again. Cheri had a huge heart for kids, but the mean things Leslie had said still hurt.

Cheri's sacrifice made a difference.

Part Four: Jonah and the Whale

"I want to come back for a third time," Leslie told her caseworker after camp. "And I want Cheri as my counselor."

Cheri was stunned. Like with Jonah, God changed the heart of the runner.

Different Person

"What story could you share about camp this year?" one of the staff asked at debriefing following Sherwood, Oregon, T.R.A.C.

Kylee, a junior counselor who graduated from T.R.A.C. the previous year, broke down in tears at the question.

After three days of camp, emotions came easily, but the tears weren't typical for Kylee. Years in foster homes toughened her exterior, and the wall she built rarely came down.

"I can't believe the change I saw in my foster sister," Kylee sniffled. "She wasn't the same person at camp."

Staff and counselors listened as Kylee described a different Savannah than the camper they knew. "Savannah's always in trouble," Kylee said. "She's closed off."

"Savannah?" Jennie asked in disbelief. She'd been Savannah's co-counselor for three years. The most trouble Jennie had ever seen was a look Savannah gave to a new counselor, but the tall pretty girl with brown hair never caused trouble.

"It's true." Kylee was emphatic. "At camp, Savannah's

softer. She trusts people and feels safe. Savannah's a different person."

Three days can transform a life when God touches a heart.

Sparkles

Dark clouds threatened the Princess Party at Kearney, Nebraska, T.R.A.C.

"Hurry up," staff relayed to the last girls getting ready. "We need to take your picture at the gazebo before it pours."

"Do I have time for sparkles?"

Beth Anne looked up into Linda's face. The mirror in front of her reflected bright eyes and professionally-styled hair.

Linda, one of the co-directors for **T.R.A.C.**_life_, sprinkled glitter into Beth Anne's blond hair. "There's always time for sparkles."

The day before, the same 12 year old refused to smile or participate in anything, including eating at mealtimes. More acronyms filled Beth Anne's application than a military dictionary. R.A.D., A.D.H.D., P.T.S.D., undefined mood disorder, asthma. Nine daily medications were prescribed for the camper who didn't even weigh 100 pounds.

An outsider witnessing the transformation in Beth Anne wouldn't have believed the change.

Part Four: Jonah and the Whale

By the last day, she even began opening up about her family situation. A loving counselor, a message of hope, a new environment and three days of fresh air and outdoor fun took Beth Anne from the belly of despair and gave her a chance to sparkle.

Just Three Days

Dear Serena,

    I am a resource developer for child welfare services. I work with foster children and their respective families. I am writing this letter to endorse Teen Reach Adventure Camp. It is not only well organized and well run, but camps that provide positive memories and experience for children that need them. Each camp offers "at-risk" kids a chance to do things they don't normally get to do. They fish, horseback ride, camp and hike. Most of all these camps provide a confidential and safe atmosphere for the children who in many cases would not be able to attend a normal camp because of behavioral or medication issues.

    Through your support more of our children can attend Teen Reach Adventure Camp. Thank you.

Sincerely,
C.G.

This Is Nothing

Izaac kicked the ground. He didn't want to go to the challenge course.

"You're probably pretty angry," Kori, one of the staff at Glendale, Arizona, T.R.A.C., observed. Scars near his temple and left eye bore evidence to the day his uncle shot Izaac in the head because his father belonged to a rival gang.

"This is nothing." Izaac scoffed. "Not like the time my mom's boyfriend tied me up and threw me in the pool."

Kori felt her heart swell. "I'm so sorry."

Izaac just shrugged and leaned against a nearby tree.

"You know, there was a man named Solomon who was blessed with great wisdom from the Lord."

Izaac slid down the trunk, and Kori joined him on the ground.

"Solomon wrote a book called Proverbs." Kori flipped open her Bible. "God brought you to camp because He loves you so much, and He doesn't want you to be angry or sad. He wants only good for you."

Izaac raised an eyebrow.

"It's true. Proverbs shows us how to live a good life and feel the love and joy God blesses us with."

The young man plucked a blade of grass. He said nothing, but listened intently.

"There's even a verse here about anger." Kori turned to chapter 22 and ran her finger down the page. "Do not make friends with a hot-tempered man. Do not associate with one easily angered, or you may learn his ways and get yourself ensnared."

Izaac nodded. The two sat in silence, the words taking root.

At T.R.A.C., Izaac heard God cared. Despite his circumstances, the young man could find freedom from the belly of anger and hurt.

Waiting List

The homely teen dressed like a tomboy waited at registration for Sherwood, Oregon, T.R.A.C. She sat with her foster mom, a German woman with a thick accent, hoping a spot would open.

Carol Joy approached the pair. Since this was the first year for Hood River T.R.A.C., the director had come to observe.

"Melanie could attend our camp next month if a spot doesn't open." Carol Joy gave the foster mother the Hood River dates.

Hope flickered in Melanie's eyes. When camp approached, however, the girl was no longer in the same foster home.

"Oh, she was only with me a week," the German woman said over the phone.

Carol Joy made additional calls, finally locating Melanie. Carol Joy's heart broke when she learned the teen had been placed in a different home every week since they'd met in July.

At camp, Melanie proved to be a sweet girl. Though she was unchurched, Melanie knew more scripture than many of the staff.

Someone had given Melanie a Bible, and she found joy in reading God's Word.

The following year, Carol Joy found Melanie in a new foster home.

When the leader at Cross Talk shared how God pursued Jonah throughout his life, Melanie stood to thank Carol Joy for pursuing her. She'd come out of her shell at T.R.A.C. and treasured her connection with all the staff and counselors.

Melanie moved to a group home just prior to her last year of camp. The home enforced a 30-day residency policy before teens could leave the premises. Carol Joy didn't give up. She joined a three-way teleconference between the social worker and the group home.

After the two-hour conversation, an elated Melanie got to come to T.R.A.C.

Recently one of the staff caught a glimpse of the camper at a store.

"Melanie looked pretty," the volunteer told Carol Joy. "She was dressed nicely in feminine clothes, and her disposition was happy."

Camp makes a difference.

I'm Not Alone

Thirteen-year-old Macey walked toward the front during Cross Talk at Scio, Oregon, T.R.A.C. "Untitled" by Simple Plan played over the sound system as campers highlighted lyrics that spoke to them.

"Everybody's screaming." Macey circled the words on the oversized paper. "I try to make a sound, but no one hears me."

One girl after another followed.

I can't stand the pain.

I'm slipping off the edge.

I made my mistakes/Got nowhere to run.

The mood turned somber as the girls reflected on their lives.

Later, Macey found Terresa during activity time.

"I'm not alone in the world," Macey confided in the Cross Talk teacher. "When you played that song and all the girls came forward, I realized I'm not the only one who feels this pain."

Terresa gave Macey a side hug. Her smile reached her eyes.

"Then you talked about Jonah and how he went the

wrong way, but God still made a way for him — it was amazing!"

Like Jonah, Macey encountered the living God.

The Song

"Keep an eye on Darcy," Debbie, the director of Ventura, California, T.R.A.C., told her staff at the first camp meeting. "She's threatened to run with several of the girls."

Debbie looked out at the steep hills surrounding camp. The Ventura camp was nestled in a ravine miles from nowhere. Nature would block Darcy's plans, but Debbie still had to be cautious. Like Jonah, she could run.

Throughout the day, Debbie checked in with Darcy. The girl played several rounds of ping pong with a volunteer named Mona and enjoyed woodworking with Craig.

The threat fizzled. Darcy and her friends were having too much fun at camp.

Darcy, wearing a set of camp dog tags that read "courage," moved closer to the stage at Cross Talk. She showed interest in the guitar, so Mary, one of the musicians, let her strum the strings.

Turns out, Darcy had a gift.

The last day, the girl who wanted to run away from camp played a song on the guitar for everyone. Darcy's smile wouldn't leave.

Christmas Present

Severe fetal alcohol syndrome made life hard for Nicholas. Quiet and insecure, he hid behind thick glasses. On his first day at Sherwood, Oregon, T.R.A.C., Nicholas looked down whenever someone addressed him. Instead of answering a question directly, he talked through Lili, the camp dog.

"Well, Lili," Nicholas would say, "I don't think I want to fish."

"Why?" his counselor would ask.

"Because I'm kind of scared of water, Lili."

By the second day, Nicholas emerged from the belly of fear. He warmed up to more than Lili. Nicholas began talking to the staff and thoroughly enjoyed camp.

A few months later, volunteers organized a Christmas party, and Nicholas' foster parents agreed to let him attend. The day of the party, messages got crossed, and the couple picking up Nicholas arrived at the wrong location.

A lone porch light shone at Camp Sherwood when they pulled up. Lili perked up her ears and sat on her haunches.

"Lili's my present?" Nicholas asked in disbelief.

"Uh, no, buddy," the driver stuttered. "We actually have to go to another facility. I mixed up the directions."

Nicholas' face fell. "But I want to stay with Lili."

"Don't you want food and presents or a chance to ride in the cart with the big Shire horses?"

Nicholas shrugged like a kid who preferred the box versus the present inside. "I don't want that. I just want Lili."

The couple exchanged a look, and he turned off the ignition.

Nicholas couldn't believe it. "We're staying?"

Lili wagged her tail as Nicholas ran up and wrapped his arms around her neck. Nicholas got his Christmas present. He and Lili sat on the porch together until it was time to go home.

Potential

Flickering light illuminated 18 faces marked with camouflage paint at Kearney, Nebraska, T.R.A.C. The boys, tired from a two-hour survivor challenge, milled around the fire pit in anticipation of the hog roast. The air was thick with the tangy sweet smell of barbecue pork.

The night before two of the facilitators garnished half a hog with citrus fruits, wrapped it in banana leaves and burlap and buried the hog over hot coals in the sand. Twenty-four hours later, hungry campers waited.

"Gentleman," Bob's deep voice boomed across the fire pit. He and his team of eight boys and four counselors had just finished crossing the rope bridge. "We're learning what makes a real man at camp this weekend." Boys stopped talking to find a seat on log benches and listen.

"A real man belongs to the family of God." Bob looked at his audience. "And I want you to know, Aiden became a member of the family tonight."

Aiden jumped up to tell his fellow campers how he had some questions for Bob and how he decided to follow Jesus. Other boys saw the opportunity to open up, and one after another, they began pouring out their hearts.

One talked about his mother in prison, another talked

about being in and out of several foster homes. Patrick, a likeable kid placed with a rural family, walked to the front. He'd given up a weekend of making good money detasseling corn because of the impact of Royal Family KIDS and T.R.A.C. in his life.

"I used to think I had to be the strong one all the time because I was the oldest," Patrick, age 15, began. "But then a youth pastor told me I didn't have to shoulder everything, and I felt this huge burden lift."

Tom, Patrick's 60-year-old counselor and a medical doctor who wondered if he could relate with teenagers at his age, was surprised at what he heard. Ben, his second camper who was a strong swimmer with a club swim team, was placed in temporary guardianship after his father committed suicide.

"These teens have so much potential," Tom said. Like many, he believed the stigma that foster teens were damaged goods. "After three days, I just want to take my two boys home."

Camp offers hope to teens like Aiden, Patrick and Ben, who are caught in a belly of despair, so these young men can achieve potential otherwise broken by abuse.

Just Three Days

Dear T.R.A.C. Staff,

Thank you for an amazing weekend and letting me come to camp for my first year. I learned a lot. Teen Reach is my favorite camp. The food was delicious — it was my favorite part of being there.

I learned a lot about God. Sunday after lunch, I asked the Lord to be my Savior. Since the Lord's been in my life, I've been reading the Bible you gave me.

I am so glad I went to camp. The counselors and staff were all so nice to everyone. I am so grateful that you all volunteer to do a camp for foster kids. I made a lot of new friends quick. I didn't want to leave. The dogs were so cute.

I really like the photo albums. There were some neat pictures and stuff in it. Thank you for my c.d., bracelets, backpack and Bible. Thank you for everything you did. T.R.A.C. is the best, and I can't wait to come back next year.

Kaylee

About the Author

After reading Louisa May Alcott's *Little Men* as a preteen, Angela knew she wanted to write and help kids in some way. *Just Three Days: From Heartbreak to Hope* melds her two life passions. Formerly a middle school teacher, Angela and the love of her life, husband, Will, co-direct Kearney, Nebraska's Teen Reach Adventure Camp. The longer they work with at-risk teens, the more they dream of touching more lives through T.R.A.C.

In addition to working as a freelance writer for Good Book Publishing, Angela has been published in *Clubhouse* magazine and *A Cup of Comfort Devotional for Mothers*. Daughters, Meghan and Keely, and stepson, Blake, bring much joy and inspire many stories.

GOOD BOOK
PUBLISHING

www.goodbookpublishing.com